Life behind the Chair

Alesia Lester

ISBN: 978-0-692-57228-3

Design and Layout by Mr. Michael J. Matulka of Basik Studios (*www.gobasik.com*)
Omaha, Nebraska USA

Edited by Ms. Lena Riley
Omaha, Nebraska USA

Published by Concrete Rose Publishing Company
Omaha, Nebraska USA

Printed in the USA

Dedication

My son, you have filled my life with unspeakable joy. You loved me even when I didn't understand how to love myself. You have taught me things about myself that I otherwise would not have learned. Your bravery, personality have carried me all this way. My only hope has been to make you proud. You are my muse. My real love.

Acknowledgements

I thank God for this fantastic opportunity to release what has been growing inside of me. I pray for continued success and humility. To everyone that has taken the time to encourage me along this journey, I appreciate you.

A special thank you to my entire clientele for listening and pouring into my life, for trusting me to glam your hair, and make your days brighter.

A huge thank you to LIFE for feeding me the wisdom needed to complete this task. My true wealth comes through knowledge.

Thank you to my family for trusting my heart with this project. To my husband, thank you for not letting me sleep until I had every word written. My mentor, P.B. I'm grateful to you for helping me find my voice. To my two beautiful nieces Chelle and Dani, thank you. To my son, thank you for simply loving all of me.

To all involved in the creation of this blessing, the editors, designers, photographers, and printers, and more, from the depths of my soul, thank you.

Table of Contents

Preface

Life Behind the Chair, Alesia Lester courageously shares her story to find and keep herself. She bravely walks us through her emotional journey into self-freedom and self-respect from adolescence to adulthood. Seeking love through promiscuity and meaningless relationships altered Alesia's life plans. Subsequently, her choices landed her in the position of teen parent, facing her immaturity, working through many hardships with self-identity, and forgiveness.

Although Alesia encountered challenges from conception, will she be able to discover that God saw something much greater for her? Will she fight the odds stacked against her to exude the beauty the beauty of a concrete rose?

Building and branding herself from the bottom to the top, she's what I call "Concrete Rose." I admire her beauty and her ability to remain humble. With her hilarious sense of humor, she makes any day better! People have always said she was "wise beyond her years." I believe so as well. Each week as I sit in her chair and listen to her stories, her life, her misfortunes, her triumphs, she continues to draw me in. She gives you her all the good, the bad, and the ugly.

Alesia has a genuine soul and forgiving heart. She has helped me understand that biological doesn't always mean better, and that forgiveness will save your life. She had the courage to tell her truth and spoke for many who have lived in silence for much too long. I have been her client for 19 years, but she has been a friend since the day I sat in her chair.

- Friday Client

Introduction

This book is written to reach the lives of young ladies who are walking in what used to be my shoes. Maybe she's been told that she wasn't worthy, was expected to fail, was abandoned as a child, lives a promiscuous lifestyle, or battles low self-esteem. Maybe there is a know-it-all teenager out there that feels as if no one understands what she's going through, so she's contemplating ending it all. Let's get a bit deeper and address the teen mother whose fun-filled childhood came to a screeching halt, due to her "adult" actions. A girl involved with a teen father who never had his father to provide him with the guidance and tools that it takes to be a man or show what it means to take on the responsibilities that accompany the title of "father." What about the young adult that had to overcome adversity, even when she knew that it would cost her pride? Lastly, what about the woman that now accepts who she has become, and lives each day praying for the little girl that she once was?

Each of these young ladies is paramount to me because, at one time or another, I've had the pleasure of being HER. I spent a large part of my life hating myself. Why? It seemed like the right thing to do considering the life I had. The pressure of letting so many people down led to countless nights of beating myself up. I hadn't learned the proper way to forgive. However, forgiveness became such a powerful tool in my life!

Realizing that I had to forgive to heal was such a refreshing moment, but it was a process. At first, I believed that forgiveness was for the person that caused the hurt or violation. I learned that was the biggest misconception. In reality, forgiveness is for yourself to move forward in your life, and reclaim what truly belongs to you. It is at that very moment that you begin to live!

I encourage you to have a seat, relax, let your hair down, and get ready, as I share with you my *Life Behind the Chair*...

Chapter 1

Finding the Courage to Begin

Find your voice and use it,
or live in silence forever.

One may think that as much as I love to talk, writing this book was a breeze. Nothing could be further from the truth. It has been one hell of a process. It all started on a Monday. I was interacting with friends on a favorite social media site. I received a private message notification from one of my contacts. He and I had not had much interaction before this moment. However, I was familiar with the seeds he'd planted in our community, books he'd written, and the time our sons spent together in middle school.

The message he sent read, "Wow, you are a great writer. You should write a book."

I stared at it for a minute, shocked to have received a message from him in the first place because of his status. Laughter was my first response. I didn't laugh because he said I should write a book, but because writing a book had always been a thought of mine, and he was basing his statement off of my hilarious posts on social media each week.

The more I thought about it, the more I realized that deep in my heart, there has always been a book with many chapters; layers if you will, ready to be given to the world. Writing a book wasn't in my plan. I wasn't sure anyone would relate.

As I processed his words and worked through growing my courage, I began to worry. I thought that the consequence wouldn't be worth the benefit. I worried that the consequences of exposing the truth of my life would be worth the benefit of helping other people. After all, I came from a family raised on, "What happens in this house stays in this house." I decided to write.

Within an hour, I had sent him seven short chapters. What I sent him was not filled with the laughter he may have expected. Instead, it was a story filled with hurt, challenges, scars, shame, love, and triumphs. I wrote from the heart, hoping I hadn't disappointed him. Little did he know that what I needed to write was much more. I shared a brief part of my story with him, and the challenge was on!

After reading what I had sent him, he asked for more. I was all ready to deliver, but had forgotten one thing; I was not a writer. I'm a talker! I thought to myself, "What in the hell did I get myself into?" I spell things wrong. I use horrible grammar. Hell, I even use run-on sentences.

His response to me was, "If you want this, you will do it."

I sat on my ass for a few months. He moved away, but still managed to check-in with me from time to time. He didn't have to do that, but it proved that he was like many others that believed in me.

I have been called a "role model" many times. It's crazy to me because all I ever wanted was someone to look up to my damn self, and here I am that very thing for other young ladies. My goal was to be a role model for my son, not others. I'm thankful because I was under the impression that role models were supposed to be perfect; without flaws, baggage, nor scandalous background.

Either the criteria changed, or it was simply a myth planted in my mind by those that wanted a spotless façade. Well, I'm here to tell you that Alesia has been dirty many times. I was drug through the mud, counted out, shunned and considered an outcast by those I once admired, boxed into social groups, and more. Those things didn't change the goodness that I have in my heart. I've grown to realize that "hurt people, hurt people," so why not me?

I had many fears of writing this book; one of them being not to hurt anyone by telling my story as I remembered it. I wouldn't intentionally do anything to discredit what anyone has done when it comes to how they've played a part in my upbringing. Everyone gave me what I needed to succeed and survive even though it may not have been in a conventional way, but who's complaining? I merely needed to purge each and everything that has been inside of me for all of these years. The good, the bad, and the ugly. These obstacles have made me who I am today. If my story can help anyone else, then my job is done. I needed the world and more importantly, my community, to know the innermost being of Alesia Lester.

I could not have chosen a better time to do this. My son has graduated and entering manhood. All he has ever known was "Mommy", but now he will know me! I'm putting my best foot forward and delivering a piece of myself to the world! Finding the courage to begin applies to each area of your life. You'll never know what could have been if you don't at least try. I refuse to continue putting off until tomorrow, what I could have done today.

I remember being in relations that started off amazing, but by the middle, it had drained me both mentally and emotionally. Each day, I would tell myself that I'd had enough and I'll just leave tomorrow. Tomorrow would come and go, but I would still be there trying to convince myself of something that would never be. Certain people in your life can be more of a hindrance than a help to you. If you do not learn the difference, you will continue putting off for tomorrow, what should have ended today. Right now. At this very moment.

I now live for me. By no means am I the most spiritual person in the world. Hell, I barely go to church as I should; but I know more than anything that God wants what's best for us. We just need to seek it! It's an incredible feeling to surround yourself with people who believe in you. These are the people that see something in you that others may not see. Please don't take for granted the story that God has placed inside of you. Tell your truth as you know it. With my story, of course, I felt it necessary to share with you. I have become a successful business owner, leader, well-known and respected master stylist, and a published author. But more than any title given and earned, the most important thing I've become is a mom.

I need my son, my only child to know that the moment he walked across that stage, I felt my legs get weak as I took my seat in complete awe of him. I want him to know that as he goes on to make important decisions in his life, I stand proud to call him mine. When I look into his eyes and reflect on our amazing journey together, with all that it took to get to this very point, I want him to understand that I have loved him from the moment I laid eyes on him. Well, maybe two minutes after that because the doctors told me he was a girl. Nevertheless, I am his biggest fan.

Chapter 2

Who Am I?

Biological, doesn't necessarily mean better.

From birth until about the age of three, I had no idea that I was adopted. Yes, in case you didn't know, I am adopted. It wouldn't be until I was sent back east to North Philly to live with my biological mother that I learned of this major event.

I was born on December 19, 1980, in Aurora, Colorado on Fitzsimons Military Base, unto D. Lester (mother) and D. Jackson (father), who were both in the military. Although born premature, weighing about 4lbs 7oz at delivery, Alesia Annette Lester was born. After about three weeks of age, I was brought to Omaha, Nebraska to start a new life.

My biological mother never actually wanted to be a mom. How do I know? Not only had she told me. Everyone else just said she couldn't take care of me. It wouldn't be until later in life that I found out it was fully her decision. I was protected from the truth until I was old enough to understand.

As far as I know, heroin was her drug of choice. As a kid, it was just known to me as drugs. She used drugs excessively both before and during her pregnancy with me. Drugs caused strife in my parent's relationship and resulted in my low birth weight. I learned that while dating my father, my mother made it clear that keeping me wasn't an option. She never told her parents or any other family members that she was pregnant with me, until she felt she wanted to. That time just happened to be after I was born.

Apparently, she didn't want me with them because she felt as if they had failed her in her younger years. Experiencing mental and physical abuse would cause the best of us not to have the greatest relationship with our parents. Add being a loner to those hardships and you have the recipe for my mother.

My father's military career kept him from being the father he probably could have been; leading to the decision that his family in Nebraska should raise me. He decided to speak to his mother about raising me first. Unfortunately for her reasons, couldn't do it. However, she reminded him of his older sister who at the time was only raising her nine-year-old son. She had always wanted a daughter but was unable to due to complications.

He reached out to her, let her know what the situation was, and asked if she would be so kind as to take me in. Without question, she said yes. He picked me up and headed to Omaha.

According to my father as we were leaving Colorado, we encountered a massive snowstorm. Just as we got halfway to our destination, his car broke down. As he sat on the side of the road, a truck driver appeared asking if he needed help. My father told him, yes, and the man asked where we were traveling. After telling the man we were headed to Omaha, Nebraska, without a worry, he allowed my father and me to ride with him. He brought us all the way to my grandmother's doorstep. As soon as my dad dropped me off, he had to return to his military duties.

My father remained in the U.S. Army, and my mother was "honorably discharged" soon after. He returned to Colorado while my mom went to New York to live a civilian life.

As I grew up, life was good for me in Nebraska. My aunt and her son opened up their home to me. They loved me unconditionally! Although I was young, I was told that I had a "real" mom. My aunt never left me in the dark about that part of my life, and I commend her for that. I'm not sure if she knows just how grateful I am to her for that.

My biological mother was free to call and get to know me at any time. The times that she would call me, my aunt would hand me the phone, and we would talk. My mother would tell me she loved me, but wouldn't tell me if or when she was coming to get me, and I never asked. My aunt made sure that my biological mother had unlimited access to my life. Throughout the years, my mom may not have always taken advantage of keeping up with me, but that was her choice.

I didn't have negative feelings about being raised by my aunt because I was treated just as her birth child. No one knew my history unless we told them. To this day, there are some that still don't know. While children with similar circumstances may have felt sad or unwanted, my life went on as normal. Honestly, I was probably still too young to understand what was going on.

At about the age of four, I recall my biological mother coming back to get me. I don't remember much of the details around it, except being on a plane. We arrived in North Philly to stay with my mother's father and his wife whom I will call "Lorraine." While living there, my mom was still abusing drugs and was nowhere to be found.

My grandfather and "Lorraine" had the obligation of "caring" for me. Although I was young, I knew that my grandfather's wife didn't care much for me. That lady was mean as HELL! While I was there, I was her responsibility. She would make smart remarks and make me feel like I was a burden on her. I didn't feel like her grandchild, and she didn't treat me like I was. She never had children of her own, so maybe that was the cause of her bitterness, who knows.

It all led up to one unforgettable night. I was getting ready for bed. I had on a Cabbage Patch Doll nightgown and slept with a Rainbow Bright doll that my aunt had bought me. Lorraine would bring me a glass of warm milk and placing it on my nightstand every night. I had a small jewelry box or snow globe with a ballerina on top of it beside my bed. The music it made was the most beautiful sound I had ever heard. There are moments when I can still hear the magical music, and I close my eyes to let it fill my space. It made me feel this mixture of good and bad emotions. Good, because the melody was sweet to my ears; bad, because this particular night, Lorraine entered my room and stood over me.

She lifted my gown. I squeezed my baby doll tighter. She began to touch me. Intimately, the way a man feels a woman. I didn't cry. I didn't scream. I couldn't. I knew what was happening wasn't right. My aunt had taught me about appropriate and inappropriate touches, but I thought it would come from a male, not a female. Not a family member at that. She would be the same woman that would bathe and feed me. Here she was, hovering over me for what felt like forever, holding on to my doll for dear life, wishing it would end. Seemed like my childhood innocence was being robbed right before my eyes, and the one person I expected to save me, my mother, was nowhere around.

I hated her…and I hated my mom for neglecting me. I'm not sure how often this happened, but I remember this time so vividly. I didn't repeat this offense to anyone. If anything, she became like the Boogie Man himself to me. My grandfather didn't know the trespass his wife had committed, and I had to deal with the anger of not feeling protected.

I just wanted to go back home. I wanted to go back to my real home with my aunt, who was now Momma, in Nebraska. I hate warm milk, and I never wanted to see or speak to them again. Momma wouldn't let anything happen to me.

One day, my grandfather called my aunt and told her that he felt it would be best for me to return to Omaha. Clearly, my biological mother still wasn't right. She was still so wrapped up in drugs and numbing her situation that she didn't have the mental capacity to care for me properly. The only reason she was able to take me from Momma in the first place was because there was no proof or document stating that she couldn't. Legally, she was my mother, but she wasn't ready to be a mom.

My aunt happily said she would take me back. That same day, my grandfather threw my mother and I out, along with our clothes, toys, and everything. He yelled and told my mom to pack our belongings and never return to his home again. My mom and I walked to a nearby train station my aunt sent for me and off I went. My aunt refused to let me be hurt or confused any longer.

I was back in Omaha, and a few years later, there was a signed document stating that my aunt was officially my legal guardian. It's amazing how back in the day you could just sign your children over on a small piece of paper for the rest of their life. No questions asked, and just like that, my biological mother would be gone forever; so I thought.

"Let the good times roll!" I didn't miss a beat after that. No one could ever come and tear our family apart. I had a big brother and a full-time mommy! My brother, who was nine years older than me, treated me like the apple of his eye. We played, talked, and spent time watching TV. He taught me how to ride a bike and play video games. He was the best big brother anyone could ask for and even though he was sharing his mom with me, he didn't make me feel anything less than his sister. He was like a hero to me.

My brother decided to join the U.S. Airforce. Our relationship to become distant. I needed him so much. He left at such a critical time in my life. I grew angry at him for leaving me and not coming home unless it was for a holiday or funeral. He went on to make a great life for himself and his family. I understood that he needed to do, what he needed to do, but it didn't hurt any less.

My aunt, who by now I referred to as "Momma", took care of everything all by herself. She made sure I had any and everything I needed including medical and dental care to a proper education. I was doing pretty well. I always felt like I was part of this family.

I had never met my biological mother's extended family aside from my grandfather. My grandmother had lived in Hawaii for my entire life. My biological mother had two sisters, one older and one younger, that I had never met.

I don't know what happened in my mom's young adult life that made her turn to drugs, even before getting pregnant with me, but that became her life. I often wonder if she hated herself, never felt good enough or pretty enough. She was beaten and mistreated as a child, so her self-esteem was very low. Things like this can break a person's spirit and cause them to fall apart, but I felt that her problem went much deeper than any of us could see.

My mother would call me from time to time, but I didn't have much to say because I felt as if I already had a mom, and it wasn't her. I wasn't mean to her, and I would still talk and laugh with her to keep the conversations from being one-sided or awkward. In fact, she had this ironic way of calling a day before or a day after my birthday. I didn't have the heart to tell her that was too early or too late.

Still, our conversations were difficult because it would end in a pool of apologies even though I had already forgiven her. I wasn't upset or angry that she gave me up or that she didn't come back for me. If anything, given her background, I was grateful. I wasn't told bad or negative things about her; only the truth. I was told how smart, giving, and kind she was. As a child, I often wondered what my life would be life if she came back to raise me, but that's normal. I would picture what it would be like if she took me to school every day. I wondered what our conversation about the birds and the bees would entail. As a kid, those thoughts were healthy, but I never hated her.

I was around nine or ten years old when I started paying attention to my biological grandmother contacting me. She would call; send gifts, cards, letters, and checks in the mail from Hawaii. I thought to myself, "How cool is this to have a grandmother in Honolulu!"

She would ask to send for me, but deep down in my heart, I was afraid of not coming back home. I worried that she would try to kidnap me from my aunt forever, so I never went. An enormous part of me wanted to know her, but the other side of me was saying, "No thank you."

Talking with her was cool at times, but it too came with sympathy and a host of apologies in tears. At some point, it started to get old. The older I became, the more I pulled away from my grandmother. In retrospect, I wish I hadn't, because I may have missed out on some incredible moments with her. I just couldn't keep carrying their baggage.

I wasn't on a hunt for sympathy. I thought my life was fine. We cannot change the past, so let's just go forward. I didn't feel sorry about the decision to that my biological mother made. I know she had no desire to be a parent, and that's ok. I understood and respected her choice once I was old enough. I have no idea what she was up against at that time in her life. I'm thankful to have become who I am, considering how things went.

A drug addicted mother with no parental skills would have been a got-damn disaster, so I'm good. After all these years, I still find a way to keep unconditional love in my heart for her. I know I have every right to hate her, but I was not taught to behave that way. I was taught to love people for who they are.

I had a million questions in my mind. Was I upset growing up not knowing who I looked or if we walked alike? Did I ever wonder if anyone would find out the secret of who my biological mother was? Did people know she was on drugs? Did she look like an addict? The needle marks that surrounded the collapsed veins in her arms, living on the streets of New York, begging and asking for money for her next hit. Shit yeah, all this stuff was running through my mind as a child.

True or not, no one could stop the thoughts I was having. I was ashamed to visit even New York for fear of seeing her living in an alley like on TV. There were many years when I didn't hear from her at all. During those times, all I could do was pray for her safety and hope she didn't overdose or contract an incurable disease from the continued use of unclean needles.

I would ask myself what in the world could be more important than being my mom. I couldn't bring myself to ask her to stop. I knew that it wasn't as easy as people thought it was to stop using drugs. Some people spend an entire lifetime chasing that very first high. I've heard people say that it makes them forget about all the bad things that have held them captive.

What in the world could be more important than being my mom?

I'm pretty sure that it became a need so strong, that she just wanted to feel "normal" for once in her life. That's the feeling it gave her; a false sense of acceptance from the world where a few minutes felt like an eternity. I educated myself early on in life about certain drugs and the effects, so I accepted that for my mother, the disease had won. Thankfully, as a result of her drug use, I stayed away from them. Sure I tried marijuana a few times growing up, but it didn't stick because I knew what the result could be.

Fortunately, my biological mother has gotten much better over the years. She calls more, remembers birthdays, holidays, and all of the important things. She's even supported me financially a few times. It's crazy because all of my life, I have loved her for free. There is no dollar amount on love, but I think it helped her try to mend what was torn apart deep inside of her. The heroin, cocaine, and alcohol couldn't fix that.

I had gone to the doctor one day for a checkup, and he asked me about my medical history. It was the first time I hesitated because I barely knew the answers to any of his questions. Can you imagine not knowing anything about your life? It was the scariest thing. I felt inadequate.

When you tell a doctor that you were a drug addicted baby, and his response is, "You probably should stay away from all drugs because one taste of your mother's drug or drugs of choice while pregnant could cause a relapse and possibly become addicted. Your system is already familiar with it."

That shit blew my mind. My biological mother didn't open up much about her life. I tried not to pry, but how long was I supposed to go without know the truth about me? Who am I?

Chapter 3

Identity Thief

*More often than not, we are dealt a hand of cards
that we are unsure of how to play. All we can do is strive to be
better than what has been placed in front of us.*

By the time I turned 12, my life was starting to change. I was at a new school, making new friends. One day, I was outside playing with friends when the house phone rang. It was my biological mother. Normally, I would try to worm my way out of talking; leaving her to speak to Momma, but, this time, was different. Momma handed me the phone like any other time. Nothing in this world could have prepared me for what she said.

"I was calling to tell you that the father you thought was yours…is not your real dad," she blurted out.

Although I was only 12, I looked at the phone like, "what the heck?" I froze in shock. I sat there in silence so long that eventually, my biological mother hung up the phone. I told Momma what she had said. She was pissed. Surely this was a lie. Why would her brother take care of a child that wasn't his? Maybe she was high? Bitter? So many questions were going through Momma's mind. Angry and confused because she never wanted my biological mother to come in and shake up my world again. How dare she drop this bomb after all these years?

Momma immediately called her brother, and he answered the phone. The first thing out of her mouth was, "Are you Alesia's father?" His response was that he knew potential existed for someone else to be my dad. However, he didn't know the truth himself. He told Momma that they had met while stationed in Aurora, hooked up, and found out she was pregnant shortly after.

It was discovered that my biological mother said that she had told him she was pregnant when she arrived in Fort Carson, after about 3 months to be exact. She went on to say that she did inform my alleged real father that she was pregnant before receiving orders to leave for Fort Carson, but he insisted there was nothing that he could do because he already had a wife and children. He was also of higher rank, so that was two strikes against him. If anyone found out, he would lose his career and livelihood. My biological mother followed her orders and proceeded on while with child.

Whatever the case was, my biological mother insists that the man whose family raised me isn't the father.

Whatever the case was, my biological mother insists that the man whose family raised me isn't the father. She eventually gave me the name of the man that could have been my real father. At that moment, life as I knew it was never the same. As I got a little older, I wanted to know if D. Jackson was my father. Then again, I was hesitant. If the results came back that he wasn't my dad, it would mean that I was all alone. Alone, in a state with a family that I didn't share a simple thread of DNA.

I decided to hold on to what I knew because emotionally, the connection was necessary. I had to believe that this was, in fact, my family. If not, I had nothing. From that point on, the other man was nonexistent.

After that, things became hard for me. I felt like an outcast; not because anyone made me feel like one, but because, by this time, I had conditioned myself into believing that deep down, I didn't belong. My dad had other kids from previous relationships. I tried to form a bond with both of his biological children (my older siblings). I attempted to have a good relationship with my older sister while we were younger; I always wanted to be around her. I'm not sure if she didn't pay me any attention because of my age or because she had already had a sister from her mother, but she has no idea how much I looked up to her. It used to hurt my feelings because it was clear that my dad loved her so much, but I wasn't sure if he felt the same way about me. After all, she was a spitting image of him, so her paternity was never in question. Our relationship is much better since we've become adults. It just would have been nice to have her in my life more when I was growing up. I love her.

The attempt to bond with my older brother was a little better because he didn't get the attention he needed from our father either. We kind of had each other for a short while, but his life started moving in a different direction when he started becoming his own man, with or without our dad.

There were also my two younger siblings that were raised by my father. He married their mother, and they grew up with the relationship that I could only wish to have had with him. I loved and hated them at the same time growing up. They knew him, and I didn't. Of course, it wasn't their fault that I knew nothing about him. I didn't express the way I felt to anyone. I just figured I should be grateful he saved me from my biological mother. He never sent advice. We never talked much about anything. Hell, we never even had a bond; but I loved him with everything I had in me because he was all I knew.

I grew up initially hating the military because it kept my dad away. Once an adult, I realized that he could have tried to come back home more, and get to know his kids. Momma never asked him for anything that I was aware of. She worked for everything. He bought a few bikes and things, but what I wanted didn't cost anything. Calling him "Dad" was like pulling teeth. I hated it. I still hate it to this day to be honest. We just didn't have that type of relationship. I looked at him more like an uncle than a father. I say it out of respect and because of what I feel he did for me by not letting me go with my biological mother.

I spent years trying to compare features. I compared my walk to him; my smile to his…but got nothing. The only similarity is eczema flair ups. I kept hope alive until I was around 16 or 17 years old. It was in the middle of summer, my father was retiring from the U.S. Army, and the entire family went "down South" where he lived, to celebrate. It was an awesome moment for him because he worked so hard to be the man that he'd become.

We arrived at my father's home to join the festivities. All of the family is having a good time, glad to see one another, and it was my dad's first time meeting his grandson (yes, I had a son by then, but I'll talk about that later). I was walking through the house and saw my mother crying. Her brother, my dad, had said something to her to make her cry. The protective side of me came out, and I asked him, "What's wrong with my mom?"

I'm sure I said it with a lot of concern in my voice; after all, that's my mom. Next thing I knew, BAM! A closed fist met me dead in my face. Craziest shit you ever heard right?

I couldn't believe it. This grown ass, military trained man, had punched his 98-pound little girl in the face. All I know is that I started swinging. People around us grabbed him, and I kept hitting. Now he meant nothing to me. Deep down in my heart, I knew that he wasn't my father. I didn't need a paternity test. I knew that there was no way in hell that a father who loves and cares for his daughter would ever do something like that. I felt so embarrassed and alone. People were in total shock.

I will never forget the look in his eyes after he did that. It's almost as if he had become someone else. There was no visible remorse. He must have been filled with so much rage that it was as if he had been waiting to do this. To make matters worse, my family brushed it away like it was okay. I was angry; part of me still is. The daughter that never asked for anything sent you cards, and tells you she loves you, gets hit? Unacceptable.

How were they able to go on with the trip as if nothing had ever happened? I watched in shock as Momma, the very person I was trying to protect, let him back into her life without any explanation, hurt me to the core. I was mad enough to kill someone; especially my so-called father.

I couldn't let that anger control my life. Besides, I had my child to raise. It was a blow not only to my face but my already low self-esteem. More importantly, the image of the first man I'd ever loved was shattered. My heart ripped to pieces. I felt mistreated and for the first time, I felt abandoned.

As time went on, I eventually reached out to him. I mailed him a letter apologizing for anything I could have done to cause him to react the way he did. He responded with acceptance of my apology and offered his own. My apology to him was not meant to ease his heart, but to cleanse me of my ill feelings that may have caused future harm to my soul. His life would continue to move on, but I needed closure.

I'm not sure if fathers realize the significance of their role in a daughter's life. She will go through life trying to find a man to mimic the traits of her father. Unfortunately, this could leave her feeling vulnerable and susceptible to abuse because of the love she is seeking in all the wrong places.

Oddly enough, once God told me to forgive, I began to feel love, trust, and significant again. I was free. This man saved my life at birth. I could never hate him because I loved him, however, as God is my witness, I could never trust him again. I had to leave it all in the Lord's hands. I needed to free myself.

Chapter 4

The Day I Stopped Dreaming

*The only reason my life is so dope is because all of
my plans failed. God chose this path for me instead,
so I will forever be grateful to Him.*

I was an extremely smart student. My junior high
school days were some of the best days of my life. I had great
friends. We were always outdoors playing, dancing, and just
kicking it like most teenagers. Now don't get me wrong, I was still
dealing with low self-esteem and boys not finding me attractive. I
was a "late bloomer", meaning I had no boobs, no menstrual cycle,
no anything. There were a lot of things going on within myself.

All of my friends were way past me as far as puberty was concerned.
To compensate for what I felt I lacked, I became more assertive,
outgoing, funnier, and more playful. My transition from middle
school to high school was an entirely different playing field! I went
from being the super cool homegirl, to somewhat attractive. Still
no damn boobs, but maturing in other areas. I sparked an interest
in boys and well, the hunt was on.

I dated an amazing guy the summer before my freshman year. He
was respectful, athletic, intelligent, and just an all-around great

guy. Our relationship went into my freshman year in high school. He was a senior. I was advanced for my age so we connected in ways people couldn't believe.

The fact that he was a senior made it hard for me. I knew that he would soon be on his way to college, and I still have three years to go. The last thing I wanted to do was hold him back, so I created a reason to break up.

To this day, I have regretted that decision, but it was necessary. His parents expected more from him, and I couldn't keep him from that. As time moved on, we drifted apart; far enough apart for me to notice a very nice looking young man on the third floor of my high school. I approached him, we exchanged phone numbers and talked for what seemed like forever on the phone.

We had so much in common. I started visiting his home after school, which eventually led to me sneaking out of my bedroom window to visit him late at night. We had unprotected sex and as you might imagine shortly after, a child was conceived. Just to be clear, I come from a pretty strict mom who wanted nothing but the best for me. I would lie and sneak out just to be with this young man. Having sex was the result of me, a child, making adult decisions.

I tried my hardest to conceal the pregnancy. I wore baggy clothes, would flop down on my stomach, and tried not to eat much, but my body was changing rapidly. Soon after, Momma told me to try on a bikini she had purchased for our upcoming family vacation. Although I was hesitant, I did it. I put the bikini on, and before leaving the bathroom, I held my stomach in as far as I could. I opened the door to walk out praying that she wouldn't see, or pay attention to the dark line beaming down my belly.

I approached her, slowly, and turned around to model the bikini. Looking me dead in my face, Momma says, "Hmm, your breasts seem to be bigger."

"Not to me," I replied, scared. I hurried back into the bathroom to change and breathe. Then it happened. I exhaled and threw up everywhere! Momma stood by the door and said, "I'm taking your ass to the doctor tomorrow morning!"

All I could do was slide down the bathroom door in relief. I was terrified, but I needed help. I was 15 years old and had no clue what I was about to get myself into. There was no turning back now.

I was terrified, but I needed help. I was 15 years old and had no clue what I was about to get myself into.

The next day, my mom and I went to the doctor's office. The whole ride there, I was nervous as hell. I didn't want to let myself or Momma down. I already knew what they were going to tell me because my body and face were changing, my breasts were sore, but I was still praying for a different outcome. My grandma had already mentioned that my face had a certain glow about it.

We pulled into the parking lot, she handed me the insurance card and told me to go in. She said to me, "I wasn't in the bed with you, I'm not going inside of the doctor's office with you." I could tell from her tone that she was hurt.

It felt different because up until this point; she had always come into the office with me when I had to visit the doctor. Doing the check-in process alone was new for me. I'd never been more afraid than I was at that moment. The doctor asked for a urine sample to conduct a pregnancy test. The results, along with the size of my belly revealed that I was about four months pregnant. How could I look my mom in the face? How could I explain this to my friends, family, or this baby's father?

When I walked back to the car, Momma wanted to know what the results were. I rambled on about everything else and then rolled into it, "He said something, probably, about how...I might be pregnant."

"What the f*** made you go off and get yourself pregnant? How does that look? What were you thinking? What will my friends think?" she threw question after question at me. I said nothing. I had nothing to say. I bowed my head in shame.

I was so far along that the doctor scheduled an immediate ultrasound. Momma and I drove to that appointment straight from the physician's office. Momma cussed me out the entire way there and continued to curse as we walked into the building, and didn't stop even as the appointment was happening. The moment the nurse told my mother just how far along I was, it was as if her world stopped.

I had four and a half months left. There was no time to prepare or process anything. Momma let me know at that moment, that it was no longer about me. Everything she did, from that point on, was for the baby.

I could see and feel the heartbreak from my mom. I even felt the coldness from my friends and their parents. My family was a bit upset, but my baby's father handled it like a man. He looked me in my eyes and told me that we were going to get through it together. He was the only person in my corner without judgment.

He worked very hard to provide for us, and at that time, I could call on him for anything. He knew firsthand how afraid I was. He was my best friend; which is strange, because, after about three years, all of that would change.

The school had become more of a challenge as my grades began to slip and my social life started to change. The teachers judged me. My peers talked about me. My focus, my goals, and my life all came to a screeching halt. It was unbearable to say the least. I was trying to live a regular life, but no matter how you look at it, there was nothing ordinary about being a 15-year-old mother.

It came time to deliver. On November 27, 1996, at 11:23 pm, my son was born. He arrived weighing six pounds, fourteen ounces, after 21 hours of labor and an emergency C-Section. I was now responsible for someone other than myself. I was confused. This child didn't come with instructions. I was still a child myself. I felt alone. All I wanted was Momma, but she was hell-bent on giving me tough love.

Of course, I had lots of help and support, but no one could understand how I was feeling inside. Although my son's father was there, my son had to come home with me. Trying to focus on school, make bottles, read books, change diapers, meet with administrators, all while being late to WIC appointments…this can not be life.

I was so overwhelmed that I gave up on school. There was always something to give or turn in, and I just couldn't keep up. I felt like I couldn't do anything right. I would give two missing assignments, only to be told by another teacher that I was missing four more for a different class. I allowed my pride to get in the way. I cared too much about what others thought of me. By senior year, I'd had enough. I chose to quit because I couldn't deal with the pressure. Of course, it was the dumbest decision I'd ever made. Then again, what's done is done. Pushing forward was my only option after making that decision.

My relationship with Momma became terrible. It was to the point where she didn't like me, and I didn't care much for her. I'm not sure how it got to that point, but it was bad. It could have been her dealing with this ever happening in the first place or feeling disappointed in me since she wanted so much more for me.

The constant arguing, belittling, and verbal abuse were killing me. I'm an emotional person, so words hurt; especially coming from someone I loved so much. I spent a lot of time trying to show her just how much I loved her and how sorry I was for all of my mistakes. I went so far as to reach out to other members of my family hoping they could help me understand why I felt like she hated me. The only thing they suggested was to pray. Even still, it never seemed like it was enough.

I remember the evening I contemplated suicide.

I remember the evening I contemplated suicide. I had decided that at around the age of 18 my life was becoming too much for me to handle. It wasn't just the situation with my mom; it was everything. I'd had enough. I felt like maybe my mom's anger would go away and she would be much happier if I weren't here. Maybe her taking me in was a bad idea and killing myself, would give her life back to her. My brother never gave her any issues, so clearly I was the problem. I had made up in my mind that my son would have a much better life raised by someone else who didn't mess things up as much as I did. I didn't love myself at all. I was ashamed, embarrassed, a liar, and a manipulator, but I hid it well.

That night, I gave my son a bath and laid him on my mom's bed. I played with him to see his smile, rubbed his hair to help put him to sleep, told him how much I loved him, I kissed my child in hopes that it would be my last time and went downstairs to shower. I knew that I was going to take my life that night. I showered, cleaned my room, and got my son's bag ready for daycare the next day.

Momma had always taken medication for different health complications, so I picked a bottle of pills from the hallway closet, cuffed them in my hands from anyone's sight, and made my way back to my room. I took one pill. One pill turned into two. Two pills turned into four. Four pills turned into too many to count. I prayed God takes me in my sleep, that way I felt no pain. Lying there, very still, waiting to die. Begging God to forgive me for all that I had done and to please make sure my son knew that his mother only did what she thought was best. I then cried myself to sleep.

The next day, as I could feel the sun peeking through my bedroom window. I could faintly hear the word, "Boo," which is the nickname that my mom calls me. "Boo," she called out again. I slowly got up to answer, but as I'm about to answer, I couldn't help but think, "Aw shit, don't tell me that she's here in hell with me?" then next thinking "Why ain't I dead?"

Then it hit me. He wasn't through with me. Just because I had given up on myself didn't mean that He had!

I was upset with God for not taking my life, and then I had the nerve to pout about it. Then it hit me. He wasn't through with me. Just because I had given up on myself didn't mean that He had! I pulled myself up out of bed, held my head up, and kept moving. I knew that things wouldn't change, but I also knew that dying wasn't the answer.

Momma is the type of woman that is strong-minded, very opinionated, and stubborn. I was no saint, but if I didn't know anything else, I knew I loved her. It's amazing how I would pray every night for God to show her my heart, but she never saw it. She loved my son unconditionally, and sometimes, I just wanted her to hold me as she held him. I wanted her to kiss me as she kissed him. More importantly, I wanted her to look at me with that light in her eyes like she did for him. It wasn't there.

I tried expressing my feelings to her, but she had a way of making me feel even smaller for feeling them, or making me feel like a punk for crying. Her harsh treatment hardened me. A part of me started to care less. Still, I would seek her approval. I valued it. I needed her unconditional love!

Her love, although tough, helped shape my future. In some ways, this was good; other ways, not so much. It affected my intimate relationships over the years. I became the aggressor. It allowed me to be in full control of where the situation headed. I could get out of a situation before things started to get too serious. I would create rules for my relationships. I would treat my partner as if losing him were nothing, because my emotions wouldn't let me fall for him. It was easier to deal with things this way. It was also lonely.

I would spend so much time trying to shape my world, which I was missing out on true love. I was too afraid to show my heart for fear of having it pushed away, the way I felt Momma had done to me years ago.

It's crazy how we allow the people we love to hold so much power over our lives. Everything Momma taught me was for my sake. I may not have seen it then, but I know now. For that, I thank her.

Chapter 5

The Naked Truth

*I've always believed that God has a way of speaking
to me through my dreams. This particular dream would almost
ruin my life, but He stepped in and gave me beauty for ashes.*

For about eight years, I would have this reoccurring nightmare. I was in high school, completely naked, but no one seemed ever to notice that I was naked beside myself. As strange as it seemed, everyone treated me as if I was fully clothed. I knew something just wasn't right, though! I carried a book bag, tried to cover myself with it, but it never helped. I was ashamed. I continued to have this same dream a lot. I couldn't shake it, and couldn't make sense of it.

I was watching Oprah one afternoon, and the show was about forgiveness and healing. I'm sitting there thinking to myself, "Okay, typical Oprah show," but as I watched, I gathered information. The next day, after placing my child inside of his daycare van, I went to the bathroom, looked myself in the mirror as I undressed. I had no make-up, no clothes, and no audience. It was just me.

I began to weep like a newborn child. For the first time, I said, "Alesia Annette Lester, I forgive you from the bottom of my soul." I screamed it through my tears, fears, and shame.

Honey, I was finally FREE! Free from the guilt that I had carried with me since I'd gotten pregnant. I released it that morning. It felt as if a ton of bricks fell off of my shoulders. To think, I had spent all these years, beating myself up over something that God had forgiven me for, long ago!

I cried the ugliest cry I could find. I knew that it would be my last time complaining about that situation. Today, I'm able to smile each and every day. I know my worth. I also realized that being "naked" in the dream symbolized the shame of having a child at the tender age of 15, lack of motivation, dropping out of high school my senior year, disappointing my family, and the fear of being judged by my peers.

Life makes little room for regret. I have none, and neither should you. Your life is your testimony.

I haven't had that dream again since. Life makes little room for regret. I have none, and neither should you. Your life is your testimony. Own it! Don't make an excuse; instead, make a way! As you read further into this book, I will let you into my world. It's not a solicitation for sympathy, but for a glimpse into the life of a little girl, with all the odds stacked against her. She was expected to fail and live a life of uncertainty. While making mistakes, I also made a promise that once I was able to stand on my own, no one would be able to knock me down. Trying to stand tall, was harder than it looked, especially dealing with self-hate. But, once you get the strength to rise above, the sky is the limit.

Chapter 6

Never make Excuses

*The more grateful we can be for the life that
we currently have, even if you don't have very much,
the more rewards, you will receive. The more you complain,
the poorer you will become. Gratitude is riches,
and complaint is poverty.*

Trust me on this one

I was feeling pretty damn good about myself. I was creating more "YES "moments in my life. My son was in school. I was an active PTA mom, sending my son to some of the best schools around, both public and private; and I worked hard. My career as a stylist is at an all-time high, my peers respect me in the industry, I am young and seasoned, and I love it. I'm working in grand salons with wonderful people that I can draw from, attending church regularly, moved into my first home; bought a new car… your girl had it going on!

With my past, and what I had become, excuses were not allowed in my home. I stand firm on that because I have taken full responsibility for my life, and all that has come with it; the good, bad and ugly. I raise my son to know that things will happen in his life, but it's how he handles them that defines his character. I tell him to let people talk. It just means you're doing something right.

As a mother of a teenage son, it bothers me to know that I can't protect him from all of the hurt and pain of this world.

At 15, the Lord knew that my life was spiraling downhill fast. I honestly believe that my son was placed in my life to save me from myself. He has my personality and smile. This young man has taught me responsibility, the true meaning of loyalty, how to respect myself, how to conduct myself as a lady, and more importantly, the art of true love.

Loving him has become my primary focus. A lot of my time was spent being a single woman (by choice of course). In my line of work, I've watched plenty of women (some of them friends), choose a man over their child. It's extremely disheartening to see this happen. After witnessing this several times, I made a promise to myself to never choose anything or anyone over my child; especially a man or drug.

I come from a family that was torn apart by the effects of drugs. I've never had the desire to use them. As I said before, I needed to understand why they were so important to my mom to take her attention away from me. I came to realize that she was battling with something much stronger that an addiction. It had grown into a disease, an illness if you will. Even on her best day, one hit could make her the weakest link. Drugs consumed much of her life. I just prayed for her. If she stopped, she stopped. If she didn't stop, oh well.

> *I couldn't miss something that I'd never had.*

I couldn't miss something that I'd never had. I recall thinking to myself, what if one day I received a call from my biological mother's family telling me that she was found dead? How would I feel? Would I cry? Would I attend the service? I honestly didn't have an answer. Where would the tears come from? Even though I hold no resentment for my biological mother, the fact remains that I never grew up with her, so I have no idea how I would feel. I'm sure you can understand.

I hadn't seen my biological mother in over 20 years. That side of the family was having a family reunion, and there was a plan for us to meet. This gathering was crazy to me because it would be my first time meeting my biological grandma, great grandma, and aunts. It would be my third time ever seeing my biological mother.

My stomach was in knots. My mind was all over the place. "How does she look? After all, she is a junkie," I wondered. My thoughts continued to wander. Do I look like any of them? Will they like me? Thought after thought came into my mind.

Finally, the day had come, to meet my biological family. I decided to take my son so that he could meet his biological grandmother, and so that she could meet her only grandchild since I am an only child. She wasn't playing when she said that she didn't want kids. She never went on to have other children. At one point, she'd even chosen an alternative lifestyle. My son was a bit confused, but he just rolled with it.

I wanted him to see his family. He's only known one side. I too was afraid, so I needed him. We got our things packed and headed to the airport.

As the plane took off, headed to Columbus, Ohio, my mind went away with it. It took me to the same place it did as a child. A picture painted of my biological mother. It was of a beautiful, goddess-like woman in a long, flowing dress, with long, fine hair, laid to the God's honey. Yes, I've always had an incredible imagination!

Once the plane landed, reality set in. We exited the plane and started walking through the terminal. I was dressed from head to toe; designer luggage and all. There was no particular reason for it all, but I just needed them to see that I had done pretty well for myself, without their help. More importantly, I wanted them to see that I was nothing like my biological mother. I had made it.

We navigated our way deeper and deeper into the crowd until we came upon a group of women. Although I recognized some from pictures, I still needed to be sure. As we approached, there stood my aunts, great-aunt, and grandma. I thought to myself, "Wow, it's real."

Every card, picture, and word, became real after 26 years. I met another set of the family that I didn't even know. Don't get me wrong, I was excited to see them, but the key players were my biological mother and grandma!

We hugged, kissed, and hugged some more, but I still felt the "sympathy" card played, and I hated it. Just accept and understand that my life was a good one. Of course, I had a few bumps along the way, but it was nice.

Once I had seen and met almost everyone, it was time to see my biological mother. She didn't fly into Ohio like the rest of us. Instead, she took the bus from Brooklyn, New York. So, off to the bus station we went.

It felt like the longest ride in the world! I let my mind wander yet again. Now, instead of her looks, all I could think about was the type of hug she would give me. Would it be like a Cosby Show reunion type hug? Or better yet, would it be the hug a mother would give her child that she hasn't seen in over 20 years? This was nerve-wracking because there was no way I could know, but I was sure that it would feel great to be in her arms.

"We're here," said my great-aunt. Holy shit, I thought to myself. My stomach was in my throat, my palms were sweating, and my eyes were burning. We got out of the car, walked up to the bus depot, and awaited her arrival. It seemed as if millions of people were just passing by me, but baby, in my wildest dreams would I have ever expected what was next.

I saw her face. It hadn't changed much, but it damn sure wasn't like my dream of 20 years, and I was okay with that. Her thin hair combed back, her face weathered, and her frail body hid under layers of oversized clothes. She had always been pretty skinny from what I knew, but as she walked toward us, she seemed much smaller than I had remembered. I know she had a pretty dope style about herself. She was neat in appearance, but it was obvious that life had caught up with her.

Now it was time for the hug. This was my moment. This interaction was going to separate the good from the bad. Here it comes...and just like that; it was gone! Yep, if I had blinked, I would have missed it my damn self! It had to have been one of the most disconnected hugs anyone has ever received. I was hurt. It was as if I were a kid all over again, and she gave me nothing. I never felt so empty in my life.

I was able to pass the tears off as "happy" tears, but I know my face showed something different. I felt broken. I was ready and willing to accept her, love her, want her, but it wasn't in her to give. It was at that very moment that I knew I would probably never see her again. I was okay with that. Never would she get another chance to hurt me.

"How dare you do me like this," I thought to myself. "You heartless bitch," my thoughts continued, but I'm a fighter, so I went on with the trip. Know that I'm on fire at this point, though.

We arrived at the home of my great-grandmother. She suffered from a few illnesses such as Polio, which confined her to a wheelchair. I'd never seen her before. I had, however, spoken with her once or twice via phone. They didn't tell her that I was coming as a surprise. For the reveal, everyone gathered into her room and told her they had a surprise for her.

I walked into the room last and sat by her bed. She looked at me, not in a strange way, but in a relieved sort of way. They asked her if she knew who I was. She replied with, "Yes," as if she had waited all these years just to see me.

I gazed upon this little, fair-skinned lady. Studied her face; held her hands, and that's when I felt apart of them. She told me my name. She embraced me when my mother couldn't. My great-grandmother, who had never seen me before, was able to hug me and show me, love. Reality set in that the woman that had given birth to me was so disconnected from me that she couldn't even hug me. I was hurt. Another round of rejection.

We spent time meeting all of our family. They are all from cities in New York; White Plains, Rochester, Brooklyn, Bronx, and so on. My mother still lives in New York. She's so East Coast! I love her accent. It's so dope.

During this trip, I was surrounded by my roots, and I must say, it felt pretty damn good. I did not let the experience take anything from away from my Omaha family because there was no doubt that it was home. It's just so hard to wake up each day and not know where I get my smile from, my laugh, my walk, hell, even something as small as my lips. I just needed to know; and although I may not have been sure of who my father was, I studied his looks too. Once the seed of doubt is planted in a person's mind, they'll run with that forever. So I stopped studying because I no longer wanted to know him.

After a day or two, I was ready to go, but I was hanging in there. My biological mother had, of course, met my son, but he told me, "Okay, she's nice and all, but my real grandma lives in Omaha!" and he was right.

Eventually, everyone decided to leave my mother and me alone in the hotel room. I'm sure they thought we could talk or bond, however; I had already expressed my feelings to my Aunt Gail about how hurt I was about the hug my biological mother gave me. I mean, everyone could feel how cold it was.

On a side note, Aunt Gail, or Aunt 'G' as I would call her, is my mother's oldest sister. A very classy and sophisticated woman! I swear she is an older version of me. She always understands me and my feelings with my mom.

The next day, my mom and I are in this hotel room, and after some time had passed, in silence, my mom says in her thick New York accent, "Aye Alesia, I want to show you something okay?"

I'm thinking, Why in the hell is she talking to me? Because I was raised respectfully, I said okay. As I go to sit near her, she reached into her luggage and removed an old, beat up and dusty bag and tells me to open it, I pulled out a hospital identification band. I looked at the band and noticed it had information from my birth on it.

Honey, you could have bought me for a penny! Tears streamed down my face into my lap. I couldn't believe it. She did care! My mother has slept in homeless shelters, rooming houses, her car, and out on the streets of New York. Throughout all the drugs, moving, and wandering, she managed to keep this small band with her for 26 years? God is awesome. Even while writing this, I have to shout because I wanted to hate her so much for not giving me the type of hug that I longed for, but all along, she was carrying me in her heart!

Sometimes, people don't love themselves, so they can never find it within themselves to love to love you.

Sometimes, people don't love themselves, so they can never find it within themselves to love to love you. I believe this was the case for my mother. She simply couldn't give me what she didn't have. For that reason, all was forgiven. She too had been carrying the baggage of guilt and shame, just like me, when God had forgiven us long ago. I've always told her that I love her and that I thank her for placing me with my aunt. I was provided a high life.

Throughout the years, Momma and I have had our ups and downs, disagreements, and disappointments. We've even come close to having some knockdown, drag-out fights (she would have won of course), but each and every day, she was there. She never let anyone railroad me. I didn't understand it then, but as time goes on, it becomes more and more evident.

When my son and I arrived back home in Nebraska, I decided to write my biological mother a letter expressing what I had felt for the last 26 years. I was pissed and needed her to know it. It was my release. Besides, I had my things to carry. There was no reason for me to tiptoe around her while holding on to her guilt as well.

She typically responds with such lovely handwriting, that it still blows my mind each time I receive something from her in the mail. I can't help but stare at her writing on the front of the envelope before opening it. This particular time, I didn't even pay attention. I wanted to hear what sorry ass excuse she was going to give me to explain why she had to hug me the way that she did and treated me so coldly!

She only told me the truth. She said she didn't know what to say or how to approach me due to the shame and guilt of not being responsible for the beautiful young lady I'd become. She accepted full responsibility for not being able to embrace me because she was empty and had nothing to offer me. At that time in my life, she was right. I had faced so many obstacles by that point, there was nothing she could say; but damn, she could have at least tried.

I could have been that woman who as a result of her childhood, left with a fear of abandonment, rejection, have trust issues, and more. Luckily, I refused to let anyone or anything live rent free in my mind or heart. I'm a lover by nature, and I will not change that about myself. I'll simply find someone to love me just as much. I walked away, learning not to allow anyone to take my joy, and realizing the real meaning of forgiveness.

Chapter 7

Pretty to be Dark

I have never seen color.

I see people

I embrace people

…And I AM NOT pretty to be dark,

I'm pretty because I'm ME…

Just like being light-skinned never made anyone better,
but it has made them uncomfortable regarding fitting in

We didn't choose our skin

But we can choose how we love one another

Melanin is only important because of ME.

Being part of a world that puts an emphasis on how pretty I was, even though I had darker skin, was crazy to me while growing up. It was almost as if it was impossible for anyone to see a naturally beautiful dark-skinned girl, so they had to speak on it when they saw it. It was as if they were viewing a rare gem, and that was complete bullshit to me because I grew up with lots of beautiful women with a dark complexion.

I hated the fact that God made me dark. I hated it even more on top of

I hated the fact that God made me dark.

the fact that He gave me parents that didn't want me, and then, He had the nerve not to bless me with long hair! I was pissed. To hear conversations of people saying, "Who? Dark Alesia?" or "Skinny, dark Alesia with the short hair?"

Talk about being annoyed. There was only one Alesia where I was from, so why in the hell did people have to specify by mentioning my complexion? Still, it was my life.

I had beautiful, light-skinned friends growing up. One, in particular, had long hair, pretty colored eyes, and she never saw me as different from her. Instead, it was me that noticed the difference. As I've gotten older, realizing that I was just as beautiful as any other young lady; even the ones I'd admired from afar.

It took me a couple of years to develop that sense of acceptance within myself, but once I found it, I knew that there was no turning back! I also noticed that even my light-skinned crew had some self-esteem issues as well. Some battled acne, horrible scars, weight issues, biracial barriers, and they didn't all have "good hair". It was then that I realized that we all have things about ourselves that keep us down, but it doesn't make up who we are.

Once I entered my twenties, my confidence was building, and I started maturing. I remember being afraid, though, that my son, who is also dark-skinned, would encounter some of the same self-esteem issues that I had; but that was not the case with him. He said that he never felt that way. He says he has always considered that he was just as attractive as the next man. I envied his confidence and was very proud that I raised him to love himself no matter what.

Time went on, and I began to see that I wasn't quite like others. I wasn't better than anyone by far, but I started to see the world differently. I was non-judgmental, loving, caring, and genuine. I noticed that you get out of life, exactly what you put into it.

I used to tear myself down before others got a chance to. I was a target for dysfunctional relationships, meaningless friendships, and unnecessary hardships, all because I wasn't secure within myself. I felt like I couldn't do, or didn't deserve any better.

I'm so proud of who I have become. I have found that people will try and keep you in a box with them because they haven't learned how to escape the mental prison that they have kept themselves locked in. I was once in that box, but I knew early on that had I stayed there, I would also have remained a prisoner.

I am now free to speak to other women and children about being "pretty, to be dark" and my words to them are sweet and simple.

"You are not pretty, to be dark. You are beautiful because of who you are within. Pretty changes each and every day, but beauty remains forever."

"You are not pretty, to be dark. You are beautiful because of who you are within."

No one would think that I've battled with self-esteem issues. They see me dressed up, make-up done, smiling every day, and taking a million selfies. Little did they know, it took a lot for me to become this confident. I started wearing make-up to cover the shame of having sex, bearing a child at a young age, and not being comfortable with myself. I now wear it to enhance the most beautiful and confident smile ever!

If you know me, then you know that I don't judge others by their actions, because I've been there. It would be hypocritical for me to judge a person based on how many men or women they have been with, the number of children they've had, finances, personal beliefs, etc. People should check their personal "Car Fax" before speaking on other's shortcomings.

I'm a lover of all things good, and I take pride in doing so. To the woman or man that feels inadequate, just know that you have to develop the mind to conquer all things. Create your box. Don't allow what people say to dictate your world or shake your peace. You will never be able to please everyone, so stop trying. In this life, you won't learn anything from someone you envy, but you can learn everything from someone you admire.

Chapter 8

Ready or Not

Never live for your children. I know that it may sound crazy, but when you think about it, what good are you to them if you put off everything that makes you happy to cater solely to them? Kids require love, a stable foundation, positive role models, and nourishment. You can buy every shoe, shirt, pant, game system, and toy, yet they will still find MORE to want. What are you/we teaching them? Do you know that if you don't finish what you start, you are accidently grooming them to become quitters? When you disrespect elders and lack leadership, you are teaching them to become lazy, weak, and disrespectful to others.

So, finish what you start, live your dream. It's possible. Kids will disappoint you and go off to live their lives, make their rules, and you will be stuck wishing you would have pushed forward. You are the life teacher while they are in your care. Show them who they can become through your life.

- Baba (Nigerian Philosopher)

The fact of the matter is, I'm a mother. Every day I look into my son's eyes and it pushes me to do better, be better, and want so much more than I had been given at birth. Walking away from my son is just not an option. Now that I'm a parent, I couldn't even fathom the thought of not seeing him become a man. In a crazy way, it made me realize that everyone isn't meant to be parents; so why not place your child with someone who can love him or her in a way that you simply cannot.

My biological mother made the best choice with what she had, and I wouldn't trade that decision for anything in the world. For my aunt (Momma), to pause her life to love a child that was not hers biologically is awesome. She'll never understand the amount of gratitude I have for her for doing so.

I enrolled in GED classes, tested out, and graduated. That day was a big deal for me!

As for me, the game is on. Parenting alone brings about many different feelings, but doing it on your own is by far the most challenging. I enrolled in GED classes, tested out, and graduated. That day was a big deal for me, but I had to celebrate it alone. I told Momma I was graduating, but by that time, she had given up. I had disappointed her one too many times. It hurt like hell.

I didn't walk across the stage because I knew that no one would be at the other end cheering for me. My diploma was sent by mail. I scored high on my test; I should have just stayed in school, but I was silently too embarrassed to go back. I had to realize that I had made my bed, so I had to lay in it.

When it comes to my son's father, who was a year older than myself, I would have loved to hate him, give him drama, or act a plum fool…but why? Although it took us both to make my son, he wasn't given the tools actually to become the man that he was supposed to be. The fact remains, we were kids!

Sometimes in life, we just can't do what we were not taught. I won't make excuses for him, but unless you walked in our shoes, you'd never begin to understand. Hell yeah, it made me mad to raise him alone, never receiving assistance or relying on anyone. My son's father has always paid child support on time. However, the things my son longed for, money couldn't buy. All he wants, is his father's time, love, and attention.

One day, my son will become a man of his own, and he will not repeat the cycle. It's crazy because I look at his father as if he is still that 16-year-old boy. It's not because of immaturity, but that's when we knew each other the most. Now that my son is 18, I see some of the same similarities. DJ is an awesome kid with much potential. He has a smile that can light up a room. My son is shy, yet noticed. Most importantly, he is in need of the father that he loves so much but is barely there due to circumstances beyond our control.

I too sympathize with feeling abandoned but never let it consume me. Too many people were expecting us to fail. I can truly admit that I wasn't ready, but each and every day, his eyes would shine brightly as if his mommy could take on the world, for him, I did just that.

My son's father and I have now become responsible for something other than ourselves. It was time for us to grow up. Although things didn't turn out the way we'd hoped, we've had a solid friendship. We don't speak much, nor do we see each other often, yet for some reason, if he needed me, I'd be there. You weren't there with us, so you can't judge our lives; instead, learn from our mistakes.

Note to My Son:

I know I was tough, but I was fair. I was strong because I was afraid. I was loud because you were tall. I was protective because you are all I have. My goal was to have this book completed by the time you walked off of the stage, but then I realized that I had so much more to say!

Now go off into the world and make yourself proud. Be the man you that you were called to be. I have provided you with the foundation needed to get you this far. As a mom, I can only get you halfway. It is now time to let you fly. You are my love, my muse, my life, and my best friend. Without you, there is no Life Behind the Chair.

Chapter 9

My Son, the Wonder Years

*Momma doesn't always choose the right words when
expressing how I feel. I'm verbal, I know. I also know,
that words hurt. I'm woman enough and "mommy" enough
(I made that up) to say I'm sorry. It's just that I love you so very
much that the last thing I want is for you to fall. Of course, I'll pick
you up, but I shouldn't have to if you focus on being great. Your
level of great! I'm on your ass because I believe in you, and will
until I'm gone. You are my world. Never forget it. I promise to work
on my words, and you work on you. Let's get better together.*

As I've said before, I was young when I gave birth to my son
and parenting did not come with instructions. I call him my "trial
and error" child because I've made some mistakes along the way.
There are some that I could correct, and others, not so much. He
was perfect, and I was afraid, but I'd accepted the role given to me
with my head held high. I styled hair in Momma's home to provide
for my child until I was able to work a real job. With help from
my mother and the support of my son's father, my fear began to
subside. About two years later, things would change.

My son's father and I split up and went our separate ways. What
I didn't foresee, was the wedge it placed between a father and his
son. Man, we had a rough few years trying to co-parent and stay
on one page. We decided not to fight or act a fool, but there was a

lot of disappointment and broken promises. Now, I'm saying that I was "Mother of the Year", but I was the more consistent parent; there were no other choices.

His father was always there financially. Even while I'm writing this book, he has never missed a beat financially; but we all needed his "presence" over his "presents." My son would go on through life longing for his father's time and touch. I would do my best to console him, but that could only last so long. As hurt as I was to see this distance between them, I still had to press forward.

I never bad-mouthed my son's father to him. After all, I was the one that chose him. I never closed his dad out. He was always invited in. I made my son pray for his father each and every night because I knew that deep down, his father was a better man than the boy he was acting like. We were 15 and 16 years old when we became parents, so I was giving him the benefit of the doubt. I was waiting for him to mature until one day, my son looked at me and said, "I don't even care anymore, Mom. I just don't."

That statement hurt me so bad, because if only he could have known the person that I knew, the young man that at age 16 possessed a different mind, worked his ass off when everyone else turned their nose up at him for supporting his son and started off more of a parent than me.

When finding out I was pregnant, my first thought was to get an abortion. His first thought was to be a father. If only my then ten-year-old son knew that man. That young man, held his son close, rocked him to sleep, talked to him, played with him, and fed him. He did all of this while his mother was out in the club trying to shake her ass and hang with friends. Somewhere along the way, things changed. We both changed. To this day, it brings so much emotion because I loved the man he was, yet grew confused at who he'd become. Anyhow, I've prepared to travel this road alone, seeking no help from anyone and looking toward the future.

I'm now raising a young man, and it's exciting! I've had some relationships; none lasted, and some, my son never met. I never wanted my son to attach himself to just anybody. I didn't allow men to run in and out of my home because my son would one day grow up and become a man himself. I'll be damned if he becomes the type of person that doesn't respect women or loses respect for women because of what he saw a child. I chose to make conscious decisions when living my life.

By this time, his father went on to have other beautiful children. My son is proud to have siblings, yet he's upset because he knows it will take even more of his father's time away from him. Sure enough, it did, but not intentionally. I'm still pressing and trying to compensate for time unspent, birthday parties unattended, sports games unseen, and that's when it started to hit me.

How could he be what he never had? Yeah, I know, it worked for me, but everyone just doesn't get it that easily. I had to pray even harder. No, my prayers were not answered immediately. That's how God works, though! I sent my baby to the best schools, moved to better areas, surrounded him with male role-models, and a great church home. I became the PTA mom, sports mom, hell, to most of his friends, I even became a second mom. I wanted him to know that I will never leave his side. Momma will always be his biggest fan, but that would all soon change.

Around his junior year in high school, my "perfect child" wasn't so perfect. He became slightly depressed. He questioned his religion and his faith in God. He was sneaky; his grades were slipping. He became more curious about drugs and was more sexually active. I was so stressed out; I felt like a failure.

At this point, I'm like, Lord what in the hell is going on? I would talk to him daily, trying to figure out the problem. I wanted to do what I could to help. I kept him from certain friends, grounded him, took his phone, computer, and checked-up on his Facebook and Twitter accounts. You name it; I tried it!

The last straw was when he came up to me and said, "Mom, I just need a therapist. Someone who doesn't have an opinion of me or my situation. Someone who will talk to me, instead of at me…kind of like you do. I want my dad, and you can't help me with that amongst other things."

I agreed. We found an excellent therapist. This one allowed my son to be himself and not put him on any damn medication. Hell, there aren't any meds for not having your dad around! My son completely opened up to her. She was a lifesaver. Most of the time, in the African American community, we are taught not to tell what's going on in our homes or to "keep our business to ourselves." Talking to a "shrink" would have been out of the question.

When I stop and think about the amount of people that get misdiagnosed or only needed someone to talk to, it lets me know that I made the right decision as a mother. I also understand that just because they are kids, doesn't mean they don't have feelings too.

My son wasn't lying when he said that I would talk "at" him instead of to him. I yell, scream, and say very mean things in hopes of making him do better because that's how I was raised. I see that it hurts way more than it helps as my son began to shut down. I was crushing his spirits, his manhood, and his dreams. I took a step back and started to listen to him and remember that when I was a child, I hated the very thing that I was doing to him.

It was "tough love", but it was killing him inside. Little did I know, I'd become the killer. My son battled with typical young things. He tried smoking, drinking, and prescription pills. Again, he was no saint, but he's mine, and I needed to understand why.

It was "tough love", but it was killing him inside. Little did I know, I'd become the killer.

Of course, he wanted to try it, just as a majority of us have. I would also find notes and messages saying that he wanted to "numb the pain" of my verbal abuse, his father's absence, the pressure of trying to be perfect for me, and the feeling of being different in school. You should know, that my son is a pretty dope kid, with a style unlike any other, but it took a while for others to catch on to his individuality. That bothered him. He would say that he felt too white for his black crew and too black for his white crew. He was raised to love everyone. Diversity was all he knew. Still, it was a struggle nonetheless.

I fussed about the drugs. Although kids were using them throughout his high school, it was totally unacceptable in my home and his father's home also. Kids were using them in classrooms and during passing periods. I went so far as to text all of his friends and threatened their asses if they provided any influence for him to use drugs.

The last straw was sending him to live with his father. Yes, the same father that wasn't consistent, didn't attend games and pressed ignore when we called. Hell yeah, him. I needed him more than I had ever needed him before. I made one last phone call and to my surprise, he came through! No hesitation, no questions, no hassle.

Many would think that I should never have called or reached out, but again, they didn't quite know the man that I knew back then. It's not for anyone else to understand. It wasn't that he never loved his son, he just didn't have the tools to be the parent that my child needed. He only knew how to be a provider, and that's a huge difference. Honestly, I thank God for all the years he left me to do it alone. It strengthened and molded me into one hell of a mother, business person, speaker, and overall person. Now it was his turn to be the father that God called him to be.

It's a task at first, but when you raise your children to be respectful and accepting, the result is well worth it. My son now has a patient mother that of course, will still cuss his ass out, a stepmother who has lent her time and encouragement, and a father who is making a better effort to be a great parent. Again, the Lord may not be there when you need Him, but He's always on time. I thank Him for that.

It hasn't been an easy road, but nothing hurts more than looking into your child's eyes and not having a clue as to how to help him or her. As a team, his father and I are getting there. Being his mother, one of my biggest fears is that my son will end up in a situation where he needs me, and I can't get to him fast enough.

He is now 18 years old. I have to allow him to grow up and make his decisions. He has graduated, and I couldn't be prouder. I don't think my son thoroughly knows what his presence brings to my life. To watch him accomplish something I never had the chance to do is one hell of a feeling. Would you believe me if I told you that I was jealous of him? Well I was, I wanted to know the feeling of walking across a stage and making my mother proud.

I can finally feel like I've done an excellent job. I can breathe. I haven't had another child because I don't know if I could love another child as I do him. I had to make sure that I gave him all the proper care and guidance because "they" were watching. "They" being all the people that anticipated failure. I loved him double to compensate for the lack on one side. I provided double to prevent him being disappointed. I made huge sacrifices for him.

One of my most memorable moments of struggles with raising my son occurred when I moved into my first home. My lights were shut off; not because of negligence, but because I just didn't have enough money. It was either pay my son's school tuition or pay for the lights. I chose my child's future instead, and I'd do it again!

Anyway, we came home, and the lights were off. He was maybe nine years old at the time. He said to me, "Mom, my light won't come on!"

I replied, "It's okay they must be fixing something in the neighborhood, so we're going to play the candle game! Get all your stuff, and bring it downstairs to the living room. Hurry up!"

He ran to get his things. I lit all the candles and placed them in safe areas. Together, we built a fort, talked, and played until he went to bed. As he slept peacefully, I prayed until my heart couldn't take anymore. I begged God to help me. I cried so hard. It seemed like I always had more bills than money. My pride wouldn't allow me to ask anyone for help. I'm sure someone would have, but I needed to learn responsibility.

The next day, I made enough money working to pay the bill and restore the power. As I pick him up from school his principal calls my name informing me that I was given a "free month of tuition" and he wondered if I wanted to use it for that month. Holding back tears I said yes but that I had already paid, he asked me to follow him into his office, and reimbursed me instantly. God is always in control so by the time we arrived home; all the lights were back on. My son went through the entire house and turned the lights off. Curious as to what he was doing, I asked, "Why did you turn the lights off?"

He replied in the most innocent voice, "Cause I wanna play the candle game with you again Mom!" I laughed so hard!

Through parenting, I am both learning and growing each and every day.

I gathered my words to tell him, "Maybe another time baby!" Now do you see why I love him so much? Sometimes you have to do the best you can with what you have. Through parenting, I am both learning and growing each and every day.

I get messages all the time about how well I parent my son. I appreciate it more than you will ever know. It's not easy. It's like any relationship. It takes hard work, dedication, and maybe even a shot of 1800. Persistence is vital. Each day, I'm all in his face, business, and life. Why? Because he is my business. I'm his mom, not his friend. We've never confused the two.

We have the dopest relationship. He's my right hand. I got lucky because things could have gone left, but God saw different. Hell no he's not perfect, but we strive for greatness. His father may not have been in the home, but he never left his heart. I taught my son to respect his dad. I don't have the tools to teach him to become a man, but there's no gender role when teaching RESPECT. That's common sense. I can't speak for this new generation, and I don't feel it's going to change. My job is to keep mine out of the way and pray for those less fortunate.

Chapter 10

No Means Yes

*Never allow rejection to DEFINE you; instead,
allow it to REFINE you.*

Rid yourself of all unwanted elements and begin again!

A new opportunity is just ahead.

*Prepare yourself for the journey and
your destination will be on your RIGHT.*

Be the GPS of your goals!

Thank me later!

As a teenager, I endured many things. I kept a lot to myself. I've always been a private person when dealing with my personal life to avoid being judged by others. On the outside, everything looked good, stayed fly, hair whipped, and makeup to the nines; but I was a wreck on the inside.

Men told me I was beautiful, but my heart said "tramp." Older people told me that I'm wise beyond my years, but my mind said "dummy." It became apparent that I was at war with myself. There was only one place in the whole world that made me feel complete. That place was behind the styling chair.

I've been blessed with the incredible gift to style hair since the age of 11. It started with my dolls and shortly after, I was able to share my talent with my friends. At times, I would amaze myself with being able to create a look for someone simply by using my hands. I would draw styles on paper, then bring them to life. Styling hair was everything for me. I felt alive as if no one could judge me because my work was so on point!

By the age 18, a friend of mine blessed me with a free styling chair. You couldn't tell me anything! At that moment, I became a "basement professional"! It was the jumpstart of my career. Doing hair in the basement saved my life, kept me out of trouble, allowed me to care for my son, and dream big!

I was now 21, and although I had worked a few jobs, nothing compared to the feeling I got while styling hair. Some of my darkest moments became excellent memories when I was behind the chair, but I needed more.

I quit my job and applied to the School of Hair Design in Omaha. I fell in love with my craft! Even though being in hair school was one of the "brokest" times of my life, I made it through with the help of a very close friend, who was also a hairstylist. We held each other down during the toughest times of our lives. We dealt with losing hours at work, our school eventually closing down, having to switch schools, and the sting of racism.

Who would have known that four little black girls transitioning from a predominately black hair school to a so-called "white" hair school would spark such controversy? We were removed from our current school because it was becoming "too ethnic" according to management. We were left to decide if we were willing to commute 15-20 miles out of the way to obtain a cosmetology license or quit, and lose all that we had worked so hard to get. I chose to continue. Nothing was going to keep me from my dream.

Nothing was going to keep me from my dream.

Each day filled with a new challenge. Legally, in the state of Nebraska, a cosmetologist is required to have 2,100 hours completed to be eligible for licensing. That said, a portion of the hours we had already accumulated were stripped away and never recovered. We had to damn near start from scratch!

Being the only black girls in the school was crazy. We were made to feel like we were inconveniencing them by expecting an education. We were learning in the basement of the school and were not able to come up until lunch time. When we would finally come upstairs, the Caucasian clients were so damn confused. They didn't know where we came from. They didn't want us doing their hair. Some of these same clients went so far as to call us "colored." We weren't used to that, but we were stuck between a rock and a hard place. Our fate was in their hands. It was as if they were waiting for us to slip up so that they could put our black asses out the door.

It was tough to experience them trying their best not to honor our earned hours. It was stressful as hell. Nevertheless, we stayed the course and focused on the bigger picture of obtaining our license. Sure enough, we did it! Through all the name calling, smirks, strange looks, and blatant racial comments, we all walked away successful; all four of us.

I'm so proud of those chicks. Though our voices were never heard, we prevailed. By the end, we had developed kind of cool relationships with the other stylists and gained a level of respect for one another that allowed us to work possibly together in the future.

Fast forward to me at age 22. I was moving out on my own, making my rules and living up to my standards. Nothing was going to stop me! I was a woman with a career. I found an amazing salon to work in and was beginning a new, much-needed chapter of my life.

I could no longer allow people to dictate my happiness. There were certain things and people that I just had to leave behind. No hard feelings. Sometimes we outgrow people in our lives, and that's okay. Never apologize for being who you are.

Chapter 11

Giving Birth
to a Dream

I wonder if people realize that absolutely ANY and EVERY SINGLE THING that you need to be successful is already within you. There is no magic set of tools with a particular delivery date to be given to you. You possess them already! So seek within, and pull out what's ready to come alive! Keep in mind that it is life changing, so if you're not ready for greatness, it's okay. Stay where you are; but for those that have accepted the challenge, see you at the top!

"Success is what you imagine it to be. Let no one kill, steal, or destroy who you want to become!" – ME

I'm a dreamer. I dream each and every night. Until one night I had a dream that was a bit different from the typical dreams of being naked or paralyzed. This was a dream of giving birth. Now I have no idea what it's like to have a natural, vaginal birth. My son was a cesarean birth, so this was very surreal.

In the dream, I was walking through my kitchen, and I was about six months pregnant (at least, that's how it looked). I began to experience a lot of pressure, but no pain. I immediately called my doctor because all I could think of, was how it was too soon to have this baby. He said, "Breathe, I'm on the way."

Well, before he could make it to me, I pushed, and out came a tiny baby and a set of keys. Don't think about the keys right now, just follow me. The child, small in size, was clearly having trouble breathing and started to turn blue all over. I was afraid. I called the doctor back, and he said, "You are going to have to put your mouth against it, and breathe life into it." I was thinking, what the hell? I'm nervous, scared, and alone, but all I can hear is, "Breathe life into it."

I proceeded to do this, and as I'm performing CPR on my baby, I start to see his color coming back. His eyes began to open; his little hands began to move. I got excited, and before I knew it, I woke up! Just like that. I woke up confused as hell.

Mind you, a good friend of mine and myself decided to inquire about opening a salon. I'd worked in a few places before this but decided it was time to take a chance. We both figured it would be a good idea, and although I wanted my own salon, we went for it. We opened up the business, and it was going great. There were no problems, we split the bills down the middle, and we had a steady clientele. We were good!

A day or so after this dream, I received a phone call from my business partner, and she says, "If you want it, the salon is yours. My family and I are moving out of town. Can you do it?"

Without hesitation, I said YES! I knew that even though we were partners, my heart still ached for my salon. I just didn't believe in myself enough through the years. It wasn't until that dream, and that phone call, that I began to "breathe LIFE" into my situation. I gave birth to my dream!

My partner's set of keys, much similar to the set I saw in the dream, were all mine. I just had to believe and be obedient. I did, and the reward was much greater than I could have ever expected. I learned how to exercise my faith. Wanting to do it, and doing it, are two different things. I was doing it. For once, I could create a YES for myself and others. I'd heard "no" so many times that it brought me joy to finally create a "yes."

I continued to follow my dreams. I stayed at that location for the next three and half years. I was lucky to have a full staff and a great area. There's nothing like making great money, living in a grand home, driving a great car, and having my son in a great school. Life was comfortable for me.

Four years later, I was presented with the opportunity to take on another salon project. I was excited about it. It was a chance for doing business in a standalone building; historic building at that. I jumped at the idea, but what I was not prepared for, was the possibility of it destroying the life at my initial location. I couldn't be in two places at once, and I definitely couldn't continue to maintain two sites. It was taking me under. My first salon was solely my project while the other one wasn't. I tanked.

I lost my home, car, momentum and confidence. The boss that I had built myself up to be was not who I was at this moment. Ended up selling the first business and moved entirely to the second. My life changed drastically. No one knew that I had lost anything. They thought I was just on the move. For almost a full year I was driving a rental car. I had nothing and was living day by day. It was a silent battle that I was in alone for the most part.

I lost my home, car, momentum and confidence. The boss that I had built myself up to be was not who I was at this moment.

Being a person that never really cared what others thought of me, I was still disappointed in myself for going backward. I couldn't cry over spilled milk. I had a staff to look after and clients to service. Although I was making money, it was nothing like before. I had to downsize my vehicle, watch my credit more carefully, and take hit after hit as bills piled up. I could barely see above water.

I'm a humble person, so most things didn't change. It was personal for me. I'd let myself fall. I lost everything. I hated myself for so many years after that but had to stay and wait for God's word. I couldn't let myself make another hasty decision without Him.

Prayer helped me cope with the devastation and destruction. I don't know why I'm able to find the good in situations, but I believed that if God gave it to me once, He would give it to me again. I just had to find a better way to do things. Maybe I had gotten too comfortable, and He thought I needed another challenge. While I was thankful for the first opportunity, it was by far the worse one yet. More than anything, it was a test. A test to see if I would sink or swim.

Since then, I've held my head high and pressed forward, knowing that there is something much bigger than me at the end of this journey. I often laugh to myself as I listen to people speculate about my life. I hear them say things like, "Who does she think she is? I guess she got it like that. How did she get that car that she drives? I bet she takes care of all of her men."

Of course, my life doesn't need an explanation, but since they were wondering, here you go. I've worked my ass off over the years to become an extraordinary woman, all by myself. I've never given two shits about what the next man or woman does with his or her life, ass, money, or time.

Please don't miss out on receiving your blessings by counting mine. I've pulled myself up by my bootstraps many times. I know what it's like to lose everything, but I also know what it's like to gain dignity and respect; and that my friends, money cannot buy.

Don't put yourself in the position of judging others because you never know when God will place you in a similar situation. I'm not perfect in any way, but I'm a damn good person with an amazing heart. Follow the path that has been set for you. Breathe life into your passion. Allow the universe to take shape and bless you with your desires. Remember, what you put out, is what you will get in return. Humble yourself and allow gratitude to shift your world.

Chapter 12

Life Behind the Chair

It's amazing how God will set you up for your
next assignment while you're still working on a project.

I spent so much time trying to perfect one area.
I was still getting all these fresh ideas and visions that
had nothing to do with my current. So, being me, I kept the new
ideas and continued working. Then one day I got frustrated.

I realized that there wasn't anything else I could do
on that project, so I gently put it aside, all to realize that it was
not done in vain. In fact, that was the only rough draft preparing
me for the real assignment! It makes me shout to know that I have
the passion for loving, working, and feeling.

Don't be confused, be better!

Sometimes I wonder what people see when they look at
me. It's funny because they become so caught up in the outer part
of me that they totally miss who I am. They see beauty, fashion,
talent, sense of humor, and class. On the inside, lies an emotional
young lady. One who loves to no end, whose heart aches for the
less fortunate; sheds tears when others are hurting.

A girl lost when she was young; she started to take on the mindset
of a man and lie down without feeling, get up with no morals and

said goodbye with no memories. I was a cold piece. Of course, like everything, that role came at a price. It left me cold; heartless if you will. Alone; but respected. The amount of respect that I received was crazy. Guys didn't know how to approach me. For once, I was in control of what I felt. Yes, I'm sure Mr. Right may have come and gone a million times, but I couldn't risk my feelings getting hurt. I knew when to chill and eventually fade away.

I take pride in saying that I've never been a "side piece"; at least not intentionally. That was never quite my style. I knew I was cut from a different cloth. I had my share of relationships, and I do not regret any of them. I call them learning experiences. I needed to experience them to understand myself. I am grateful for them. I was a confused little girl, stuck between promiscuity and battles with self-esteem. It was clear that something needed to change; and shortly after, it did.

I spent a lot of time begging God to take those feelings and faces of men I'd encountered through my past, and He did. It was the craziest thing ever because although I'd prayed for it, at times, I wasn't quite ready. One night I was at a local night club with my girls dancing and having fun. A guy approached me while saying my name. His voice sounded familiar, but I couldn't think of where I could have possibly known him.

He said, "Hey Miss Lady, how have you been? Long time no see."

I took a step back and replied, "I'm sorry, where do I know you from?" The look on his face said it all. This was a guy that I'd had some dealings with back in the day, but keep in mind; I had just prayed for God to remove faces and sexual feelings.

Anyway, I played it off and blamed not being able to make out his face on the alcohol. We laughed about it, but to this day, I have no idea who he was. It proves that you have to be prepared for God's journey for your life. I asked for a clean slate, and so it was.

That's when my sense of humor kicked into high gear. Everything became funny to me! I realized that laughing was good for my soul. It cleansed me, as did my tears. Sometimes you have to laugh to keep from crying. I let go and have been laughing ever since. Life is too short to dwell on things that are beyond our control. So what, I've made mistakes; so have you. So what I have a past; hell, so do you!

My past has paved the way for the most amazing future. I have accomplished things I never knew I could. I am now a selfless giver, a compassionate lover, and a non-judgmental young woman whose primary goal is to stay on the path of inner peace.

> *My past has paved the way for the most amazing future. I have accomplished things I never knew I could.*

My 20-year career as a stylist and business owner has provided a zone for me. As I've said before, I'm so alive when I'm behind that chair. That very place saved me. It gives me a rhythm that only I can move to. It allows me to touch lives and meet people exactly where they are, at that moment. My clients give me life! We laugh, cry, pray, and laugh some more; and that brings me joy.

It's behind the chair that I can feed my soul, nourish my personality, and add life to my character. My life has been a journey...a blessed one. I've been through a diagnosis of cervical cancer, two emergency breast biopsies, two abortions, and miscarried, all before the age of 30.

Oh, you didn't know all of that? Well, let me take some time to encourage you. Giving birth to a child is hard on the body. Especially when the body isn't fully developed. While giving birth to my son, I had to have an emergency Caesarean. I healed up correctly on the outside, but not on the inside. I was left with scar tissue and huge cysts on my ovaries. The pain was unexplainable.

Four years after giving birth, between the ages of 19 -20, I noticed the pain was getting unbearable. I noticed that I was having pain after sex, but I was still young and didn't understand my body. I went to see a doctor about the pain, and that's when I got the news. I had cervical cancer. I remember trying to sort through the initial shock. The minute anyone hears the word cancer; you immediately think 'death.' Before any tests were conducted, I was already trying to figure out if I needed to write a will.

My mom was the only one who knew that I was in the early stages of cervical cancer. Since I was diagnosed early, I didn't have to do chemotherapy. The doctors were able to use a laser to burn it away. Except a few minor issues, I was okay. I was blessed to get through it. That experience has inspired me to celebrate with others who make it through it.

That wasn't the end of my medical battles. In 2004, I found my first of two lumps. I had seen someone on TV demonstrate how to do a self-breast exam. My boobs were so small, but I happened to raise my arm while in the shower and felt a knot under my armpit. I wasn't scared at first because it didn't hurt. I let a whole year pass, saw a commercial, and felt under my armpit again. The knot had gotten bigger and was tender to touch. I made an appointment with a breast cancer specialist for a biopsy. They found a large mass and were able to remove it. It was the size of a golf ball. It wasn't this size the first time I had felt it. I was told to lower my caffeine intake, as that can trigger cysts. Fortunately, it was benign.

While in a great relationship, with a lot of potential back in 2001, I had gotten off one birth control to switch to another, and got pregnant. I didn't know I was pregnant until I miscarried. Yes, miscarried. I was in Momma's basement washing clothes. I'd had cramps all day, and they progressively got worse like contractions. I rushed to the bathroom, sat on the toilet, hoping the feeling would pass. It felt like a terrible menstrual cramp. Before I knew it, there was a lot of blood. I was terrified. I got up, cleaned up, and called my boyfriend at the time to take me to the Emergency Room. The doctor entered the room and told us that I had a miscarriage.

My boyfriend and I were both shocked. We had no clue that I was pregnant; two months pregnant. There are no words to describe what was happening with my body. I don't typically have a regular cycle, so it didn't occur to me to take a pregnancy test. I felt helpless. I couldn't help but wonder if this was payback for earlier decisions to have abortions.

On the way home from the hospital after the miscarriage, my boyfriend and I were silent. Neither of us knew what to say. I wondered if he blamed me. It was a turning point in our relationship. He wanted to try again, while I was thinking, "I wasn't trying the first time."

A miscarriage had a different mental impact than the abortion, and I needed to heal.

We were very clear on how we felt. Our relationship got worse because, by that time, it was clear that we had different views. A miscarriage had a different mental impact than the abortion, and I needed to heal. With the abortion, I was able to process and deal with any repercussions beforehand. I made that choice. While a miscarriage, is an uncontrollable situation that leaves you to handle after the fact.

In 2010, at age 30, I went in for my routine pap, and the doctor found the second lump. She scheduled an immediate appointment with the breast cancer specialist after looking at the x-rays and sensing that something wasn't right. I got to the appointment, scared as hell because this experience was far different than the last one. I'm sitting there with the breast cancer specialist, and all I could think about was if removing this lump would change the shape of my already small boobs! She laughed at me, but I was dead serious! She replied, "No, I just want to make sure you're safe." I was scheduled for the outpatient surgery. I went in, had it removed. Thank God I dodged a bullet, it too was benign. They had to use a tool similar to an ice cream scooper. This one was the size of a tennis ball!

All of these battles helped me to remember how real God is. I stayed focused and faithful. There was no way He would take me through these things for nothing. It was hard to look at myself while going through because I was so damn "classy" on the outside but felt as if I was living a lie on the inside. Still, I picked myself up, faced my fears, and kept stepping. None of the things I went through define who I am. We all have "shit" and this happens to be mine. Love it or leave it, it's me.

Now allow me to reintroduce myself. I am Alesia Lester, one of the sharpest and dopest young ladies I've ever had the pleasure of knowing! Now who are you?

Life has a crazy way of allowing things to come full circle. We may not have been ready for some of the things that we've asked God for in our past. I have absolutely no regrets. Embrace your life and never apologize for who you are. Find your "muse." Tap into what motivates you and become the best. Life has been my greatest teacher. Pay attention and you will learn.

Yes, you will make mistakes, but you don't have to become the error. Someone encouraged me to share and tell my story. I was afraid at first. I didn't want to expose my filth, but I

Yes, you will make mistakes, but you don't have to become the error.

have never felt freer or more healed than I do at this very moment! So if you are reading this, and it does nothing for you, thank you and pass it to someone that can relate. However, if you are reading this and have experienced abandonment, embarrassment, drug addiction, unbridled sex, failure, feelings of inadequacy, and so on, please know that I was there. I understand, and you will break loose from every chain that has you bound. Free yourself. You are remembered in this life for two reasons (1) the problems you have solved and (2) the problems you have created. Ask yourself if you are part of the problem, or the solution.

Chapter 13

Who's the Boss?

It all starts with you! Sometimes we spend too much time worrying about how the next man will eat. Focus on self, believe that you will attain greatness. I've never had the desire to eat off of another man or woman's plate. Especially when what I feel I deserve isn't even served on the menu. It starts with me. I knew I was a BOSS before I became one. Not because anyone told me I would be, but because I BELIEVED that I was.

It's amazing how everyone wants to become a boss until there's no more toilet paper. This is one of the simple things that can piss you off while managing a salon or any small business. Some of the other things I hear are, "We're out of trash bags," "Do we have any more water?" "We need a new dryer," and my favorite, "It's cold/hot in here!"

Of course, as a boss, it's your job to make sure these things are in order so that the business runs smoothly. The thing that some employees don't see or understand is that even when faced with the struggle of paying bills in two places, the business must always win because you are responsible for the employees. Also, you have to consider each and every person that contributes to making the company run. As employees, when you sit under the dryers just because you're "cold", not only are you wasting money and heat, but also burning that dryer out much faster when it could be used for other clients. Allowing the water to run at the shampoo bowls to clean combs and brushes or even leaving it on while shampooing is a waste of water and money.

Cleaning the drains, taking out the trash, cleaning the bathrooms, sweeping, or picking up behind clients is a group effort.

Cleaning the drains, taking out the trash, cleaning the bathrooms, sweeping, or picking up behind clients is a group effort. It reflects on everyone, but the overall responsibility falls on the boss. Remember that "booth rent" typically only covers space and basics. Your client's potato chip bag or an open can of soda is not covered under booth rental. Now I love everyone's opinion, and they have great feedback with a list of demands, but to be successful, it takes a team; a consistent team. Employees don't see that the boss has to pay for the plumber, electrician, snow removal, maintenance and repairs, replacing equipment, utilities, rent, property taxes, and insurance. That list doesn't even include what the boss has to spend on their personal mortgage, light bill, gas bill, phone bill, car payments, insurance, and so on. I tell people all the time that there is a lot of work and responsibility that comes along with this title.

Don't get me wrong, it totally comes with its perks. You have the ability to be recognized amongst many of the businesses in your industry, you are asked to be a part of several events and community projects, your opinion is sought out during the architectural planning and growing in your community, and so much more. It also provides a platform to show other's your brand and what you're made of. It's a conversation piece as well. I've noticed that when I would say that I was a stylist, people would respond with, "Oh ok, maybe you could do my hair." But once I became a salon owner, the conversation would go a little something like this, "So Alesia, what is it you do for a living?"

I would reply "I'm a Master Hairstylist and salon owner," and that shit would go from 0 to 100 real quick! Now, the person wants to know my history, all while trying to guess my age and how I did it. I simply smile and answer all the questions they ask. It used to piss me off because I don't think people, especially those who are not in our industry, actually understand the importance of what we do and how vital we are to their lives.

A Licensed Cosmetologist, on any given day in Nebraska, has to ability to make anywhere from $30 to $500 in a day and some cases more. Most of us work at least five days throughout the week. The amount, of course, depends on the stylist and how well they market themselves as well as their repeat customers.

I'll say that I have been a stylist for 14 years, and I have never had a part time job, and surely child support wasn't enough to save my life! My life has dealt in cash and has allowed me the blessings of purchasing things I've only dreamed about. My payout comes from behind my chair and the hard work and dedication that I put into my clients along with my job. It doesn't come from the seats I rent out. That alone only pays the bills and keeps the lights on.

It's my passion and my love for my staff that keep me from doing anything else. While I sit and watch people go to jobs every day that they hate because it pays them well. I couldn't relate because I'm blessed to kill two birds with one stone. I have clients with a million college degrees, more student loans than paychecks, and deadlines to meet with a boss that they cannot stand. In conjunction with being their stylist, I have also become their confidant, friend, and counselor if you will. I love it! Speaking of counselor, I believe that no one but God places me in the presence of young ladies needing guidance, attention, and love. As I'm styling one of my clients whom I've done since she was 12, now 21 she's telling me how her life is spiraling downhill, and I see it too, I have for a very long time but each time I encourage her to do and be better. She tries, but falls short each time. Then my phone rings and I answer and it's another one of my clients telling me how confused she has become on her life path. As I begin giving her advice, the one in my chair starts crying. So now I'm holding the phone with my shoulder, rubbing her back consoling her and still encouraging the one on the phone. We then hang up and I talk deep with my client in the chair. Holding her head up and smiling she reaches into her pant pocket to scrape enough dollars to pay for her hair, I pushed it back, held her hand and hugged her tightly. That young lady cried so hard. It's not always about the money; I just want her to be good to herself. That was just one of many rewarding moments in the salon.

The flip side of being a business owner is having to learn some of the fundamentals of business. Learn to save and manage your money properly. In this line of work, as fast as you make it, is as fast as you can spend it. Build credit, buy health and life insurance because one day these hands may not work the same as they used to and you will need to have a backup plan. I watch young stylist burn themselves out early because they never had a plan. They saw the glitz and glam of being their own boss but fail horribly. Remember to work smarter, instead of harder.

Without our industry, there are no television shows, movies, plays, theaters, awards, magazines, etc. We are very necessary. That said, the show must go on, and so would a real boss. It's much more than a name or title. You become a role model whether you ask to be or not. It is important to conduct yourself in a way that protects your brand.

Without our industry, there are no television shows, movies, plays, theaters, awards, magazines, etc. We are very necessary.

Staffing is everything. You have to find a great group of individuals to work as a team. I chose to employ master stylists/barbers that could bring originality, confidence, and diversity to my business. They each hold a unique gift that the world unwraps daily. I'm not sure if they fully comprehend all that I juggle to make sure they stay great, but I pray for nothing but prosperity for their lives and families.

They take care of me, so I make sure I take care of them. They're my family, and I wouldn't trade these fools in for anything in this world. Each day I try to show them new ways to improve and go about life. Everyone isn't meant to be a boss, but everyone has a purpose on this earth. Seek your WHY in this life. Remember, being a boss can be the most rewarding title ever or this shit could be just a fancy way of saying, "We're out of toilet paper."

Chapter 14

Wise Beyond My Years

The wisdom I seek comes from those much older than my immediate peer group. Each week I sit at a tiny diner and eat amongst the elderly because these are people that have lived a life that I have yet to encounter. They fill me with knowledge and faith that strengthens me daily. Sometimes I see that a person my age hasn't lived enough for me to draw from them just yet. Even with my clients, I love them all. However, the older more seasoned clients don't realize that they leave me with much more than I've given them. Knowledge is extremely powerful. Use it wisely.

I've always been wise for my age. Momma would say that when I was five years old, I thought that I was 15. I'm not sure why I was so advanced. As I grew up, it became a blessing and a curse. It was a blessing because it allowed me to hang with older crowds and no one ever questioned my age. I spent a lot of time with older women, soaking up all their knowledge of men, finances, and life lessons. As I grew up, I dated older men because guys my age couldn't relate to me.

Early on, I knew important things such as how to keep a home. Momma would say, "No man wants a trifling or nasty woman," so I knew to pay attention to how I kept my home. I kept myself appealing to a man. She would also tell me," Never have men running in and out of your home or around your kids." No problem. I would just see them at their place or not at all.

> *"Be the person you want to attract!"*

"Be the person you want to attract," she would say. That one was awesome because I can recall in my previous dating experience, I've never dated a man that done me wrong; wrong in the sense of hitting or verbally abusing me. They may not have been perfect, but I don't recall ever being mistreated by a man. I thank God for this and think it's because I set the tone for the way I expect to be treated. If that person couldn't respect me the way I respected them, I would leave. No hard feelings and no fighting. I would just go.

I believe that both men and women have their level of ENOUGH. Everyone is different, so you have to understand your happiness to achieve it. I also knew early on that men love differently than women. I learned not to confuse this with them not having feelings or emotions because they're people too. Being a man doesn't give a woman the right to mistreat or hurt him expecting him not to react because 'he's a man and should be able to handle it.' Hell nah nothing could be further from the truth. Men feel; some more than others, but they do feel.

One of the hardest things for a man to do is just to approach a woman. They are afraid of rejection too. Most of the time, once they have built up the confidence to walk over and say hello, we shoot them down by responding with, "Nah, I'm good," or "No thank you," and sometimes, there are women that just flat out ignore them.

I'm sure that hurts, but in most cases, that woman will allow that potentially 'good' man to walk away with his head down. They're soon approached by a man who walks up behind her, grabs her waist, palms her ass, or asks if he can take her to breakfast instead of dinner. It's crazy, but if we're honest, we all have been guilty of this. I know I've been in that situation a time or two. Are you 'breakfast material' or 'dinner material'? Trust me, there is a difference, and if you can't identify the difference, you'd better wake up. Once you realize who you are, your ass will spend the rest of your life trying to find a man like the one you turned away!

I want to switch gears a bit and speak to parents and those that want to become parents. It is silly to make a man stay with a woman just because they have become parents. Being parents only makes you partners. It doesn't mean you are perfect. There are no perfect parents. Ours weren't perfect. You have to be fair. Let go of all bitterness, hate, and hurt. When you harbor those feelings inside of you, it becomes toxic. You start thinking evil thoughts and engaging in immature actions. Your children will eventually pick up on those very thoughts and will display the same energy that has held you back.

Focus on living. Each and every time you lay down and create a child without a genuine commitment or marriage, there is a possibility that you may be dealing with this thing alone. If you go into it with a "single" mind, you will have to be prepared for what may come next. Keep in mind that you two chose each other; the child didn't want you. Why would you let a child suffer because of your mishap?

Each and every time you lay down and create a child without a genuine commitment or marriage, there is a possibility that you may be dealing with this thing alone.

Money alone doesn't raise a child. There is no set dollar to how much it takes to support a child. ome mothers out there are more concerned with "things", rather than time; Jordans, rather than life insurance policies. Trust that God will provide and that as long as you stay active, everything that you ask for will be added unto you and that child. When you act ugly, you block blessings from coming your way. Be careful of the role you play. God said that He will make your enemy your footstool. Be patient. I am speaking from experience. Everything wasn't always readily available, and I won't sit around as if my son didn't have the necessities. His father never missed a child support payment, but I would have traded the case for the time, any day.

There comes a time when you can't rely on anyone but yourself to get to where you want to go. Goals have always motivated me. One thing I can't understand is a lazy person. I often wonder what made them give up and become so dependent on others. I don't want to hear shit about a generational curse. They need to get their ass up and strive to be more.

A man will respect a woman so much more when she's striving to better herself. Most men love that type of woman. Now, if they don't have much going for themselves, then they will stay complacent. A man with his own personal goals will go straight to the top if he has a woman with a like-mind. Think about it, if you have a "bottom" mentality, you will never know what it's like to reach the top.

Each time you enter into a relationship, it should make you better. You should develop better values, time management, finances, parenting skills, and partnerships. If your relationship pulls you down, you need to leave as soon as possible. If you don't, you will end up marrying the wrong mate, living in the wrong house, giving birth to the wrong kids (yes, I said wrong kids), working the wrong job, and ultimately, miserable.

I treat each relationship like a business. My ultimate goal for each of my businesses is to go to the top. This means I have to invest in the future of the company, evaluate my position, seek out growth opportunities, and ensure no one comes in and tears my business apart. Now, of course, no one wants to see the company fail, so you have to work together as a team. If you apply that simple formula to your relationship, it becomes a no-brainer.

Life can be rather easy. We just choose to complicate things. Sometimes common sense isn't so common. Take heed to the life lessons that you've learned along the way. Fill your space with people that are moving in the same direction as you. You find yourself outgrowing some people from your past, and this is okay. Outgrowing them doesn't mean you can't love them, it only means that you love yourself much more. You don't need to apologize for being who you are. Move along, and as my grandfather always said, "It's easy to be nothing, but it's hard to be somebody."

Every part of my life moves in silence. Not because of shame or secrecy, but because I believe that true happiness and or success needs no audience. I'm an "action" person. I want to SEE my life take shape and not just TALK about what I want to do. That's my crazy way of doing things.

Things are changing in my life. I'm going to change. Change is good. It's the way in which you change that creates a problem. I'm soon to be 35. I'll be damn if I'm in the same boat, tax bracket, state of mind, or shoes that I was in last year. Each year I'm better. Think about where you are and see if it lines up with where you're trying to go.

Chapter 15

Love Without Losing Yourself

Stop where you are right this very moment in your life, and ask yourself, "Does the person you lay next to at night do the following":

Complete you / Compliment you / Motivate you / Accept all of you / Nourish your soul / Stimulate your mind / Lend an unselfish hand / Sympathize with you / Brighten your day / Create a smile within you / Make you dream bigger / Operate like a team player / Keep you on your toes / Make you feel secure

If so, you're well on your way to happiness. If not, you will spend an eternity trying to right what will always be wrong, not allowed to enjoy each other's love because it's clouded with an error. Both men and women deserve the same respect. It's fair to assume he can take it because "he's a man." Hell, he's human too. Same for women; some appear tougher than others, but at the end of the journey, we all seek the same feeling.

Have you ever loved and lost? I'm not talking about losing others. I'm talking about losing yourself. Have you ever loved a person so much that you couldn't see a reason to move on, date again, let someone in, or love? If you have been there, you have to promise me that you will do all you can never to return to that kind of love. It's toxic, unhealthy, and means that somewhere along the way, you felt like you couldn't do or didn't deserve anything, or anyone better.

Don't you realize that if God gave it you once, He would give it to you again? Maybe it just wasn't your season with that person. Maybe that person was placed in your life as a "template" of what you should or shouldn't expect in your next relationship. If a person hurt you, why would you go back to hurting yourself? Seek a mate that makes you feel good, instead of evil. It's very straightforward. Pay attention to the partner that treats you well! It's basic math. I also know that the heart wants, what the heart wants.

I'm no fool; I'm more of a realist. For example, I love pineapples. I'm also allergic. My heart wants them, but my mind knows that shit does me wrong! My tongue starts to swell, my lips begin to burn, and my throat starts to itch; and yes, I eat them anyway. I also have to accept the consequences of eating something when I know better.

What I'm saying is, if you know someone isn't right for you and your life, yet you continue to try and make them stay, you deserve all of the hurt and unhappiness that comes with him or her. I know it's not always easy to walk away from what you believe to be love. I would never tell you to up and leave, however, you should understand who you are and what you want your situation to become. I see this in both men and women. Yes, men too, will stay in an unhealthy situation with women for reasons such as kids, companionship, guilt, and so on. I see women wait for security, stability, finances, and some women even stay so that the other woman won't get him.

People are willing to stay emotionally bankrupt due to pleasing others or because you think you would fail without the financial support of someone else. I know it sounds insane coming from me, so imagine having actually to live it. I'm speaking from experience. I've been lied to, cheated on, and yes, I took him back because I loved him. I also realize, that I no longer trusted him, nor did I respect him. I felt like I was held hostage mentally. He tried to regain my confidence, but I was emotionally gone.

People are willing to stay emotionally bankrupt due to pleasing others or because you think you would fail without the financial support of someone else.

Speaking of relationships, I also had the great pleasure of dating an NFL player for about a month shy of a year. He was an amazing guy. He was funny and down to earth. We met at an event in Kansas City. I had no idea who he was. Before him, I never gave "two-shits" about football. He was polite, so I bought him and a friend a drink and went on to enjoy my night. He was taken aback by the fact that someone had done something for him, even though it was small, that he came and introduced himself. I still had no idea who he was. The DJ then calls his name and the name of his friend over the mic. This man played as running back for the Kansas City Chiefs. (I will not reveal his name or years played, he is still a great friend of mine)

We spent the rest of the night laughing, joking, and talking about life. I'm such a private person when it comes to my personal life, yet we connected quickly on a crazy dope level. A friendship developed, soon to be filled with partisan loyalty. After spending crazy time together and after our families were getting to know each other, he ended up cheating. I was crushed.

I was the one person in his life that never took from him, and this is how he repaid me? He tried numerous time to make it right. It didn't matter because I just couldn't take it. I knew deep down that he cared for me. Nevertheless, he makes a mistake that would not only cost him a friendship (the woman was his teammate's side chick) but it also a genuine a relationship with me.

He would often ask me if I was ashamed of being with him. I would quickly assure him that I wasn't, but I knew something wasn't right during the season. I couldn't allow him to make me look crazy to our family and friends. Sure enough, he did with his infidelity.

One weekend I had arrived in Kansas, frequently I would stay with him. Each time I would come in town I knew where he left the house key, and I would confidently let myself in. Making my way through the house turning off unnecessary lights, washing the few dishes left in the sink and folding his shirts the way he likes them. He would always tell me that I reminded him of his mother. I was used to him not being home when I'd got there due to practicing so I just showered and made the children's beds. He texted me and said, "Get up, I'm taking you to dinner, I love you, and I'm sorry." Confused, but I text back "ok, love you too." Something was wrong; I just didn't know what it was. Then I get a call from his mother "Momma T" she was the coolest, she was a hard working lady who also battled a few demons while raising her children but she overcame them, and I was glad to have met her. "Hey baby," she said, are you in town? "Yes ma'am," I said, "well I have something to tell you. You know I love my kids, but I do not condone any wrong doing by them." Momma T would go on to tell me everything. A woman whom I had met early in our courtship, that dated a former teammate would be the woman that became pregnant by my boyfriend. Let that sink in. This woman and I have entertained one another at many social gatherings that our men would have. Our cell numbers were stored in each other's phones. Were we "besties" of course not, but we were very cordial women when we would see one another. Shortly after, he came home to me sobbing and crying my eyes out, apparently that's what we needed to talk about. Pissed that Momma told me first, he then confirmed what his mother had said. I screamed, and I yelled. The look on his face was apologetic, he pleaded with me to stay, but I took my things, drove back home from Kansas City, and never looked back. Come to find out, the baby wasn't his. And neither was I.

The things I learned from these types of relationships are priceless, and I have no regrets. I believe that unhealthy relationships are necessary. If you don't have them, you'll never understand how it feels to be in a healthy, loving, and fulfilling one. I have dated good guys, older guys, younger guys, and hell, I even dated a guy that thought he was a got-damn ninja. The point is, I needed those relationships, whether good or bad. This allowed me to define fully what I was seeking in a man.

I believe that unhealthy relationships are necessary.

Oddly enough, I have great relationships with my ex's; not because we have sex or talk on the phone, but because we do not. I do not, nor have I ever, gone back to an ex for any reason. If they're reading this book, they can vouch for that. I don't do this because I'm mad or upset; I just don't like to confuse their lives or my heart. We had our time, and for whatever reason, that time was up.

I believe that if we ever had a genuine friendship, we would always be able to find our way back to that point, and we do! My exes weren't bad guys. They just weren't the guy for me. Still, I'm optimistic. I know that we were placed in each other's lives for a reason. With the good that we brought each other, we should transfer that energy towards strengthening our next relationship.

Crazy right? Hell no! If you think about it, while you are sitting there hating him or her because of what they have done to you, that person is sleeping well, eating well, and not thinking about your miserable ass. They're living their life while you're stagnant. Don't get stuck there. Let it go no matter how much it hurt. Rebuild your mind so that it's strong enough to walk away. If it's meant to be, it will come back. You just make sure that your heart is lined up with your eyes and ears.

Loving someone more than yourself happens without even realizing it. For me, I'm a nurturer by nature. I give, I love, I understand, I clean. Hell, I knew I must've been in love because my ass was even cooking and that's not my thing at all. But for "the one", you will do all those things and more.

I was in another relationship where I was doing all of those things. As time went on, I started to notice that the man I was with wasn't the man I needed him to be. As only women can, I picked up on his behavior changes. Unfortunately, I caught the wind that he was entertaining another woman. I spoke with her, and she confirmed it. I confronted him about it.

At first, he tried to deny it, but eventually, he came clean. I was hurt. I screamed, yelled, threw things again, and even punch a glass cabinet while I was trying to hit him. I started to bleed profusely. My hand was cut up and filled with glass. He attempted to help me but my adrenaline was pumping, and I would not allow him to get close to me for his sake. I still wanted to punish him, because I was hurt.

I stood up, gathered myself together, and went into the bathroom. Behind that door, I cried so hard that I made myself sick. I made him leave, and as I cleaned each tiny piece of glass from my carpet, I saw that I was merely picking up the pieces of my life. I threw every piece away. It wasn't good for me anymore. With my hand still throbbing, I tried to gather my thoughts. I promised myself that I would never be taken to such a point again by anyone.

That was in 2004. It is now 2015, and although I cannot say that I haven't gone through heartache or upset by the actions or lies of a partner, Honey, I stood true to my word that I would walk away before I let someone bring me down to their misery. Now, I leave. It doesn't mean that I don't know or understand love. What it does mean, is that people have been confused for so long, that they start to believe that hurt is the only way to identify love. Nothing could be further from the truth. Real love doesn't hurt. Sure, it has its trying moments, but it shouldn't make you feel depressed, less than, inadequate, unlovable, or even physically hurt. At least not the love I know.

Each day at work, I encounter at least one woman that says, "I'm going to cut all my hair off! I'm going to start living for me. I'm changing my life," and every time I hear it, I laugh. Number one, they should have already been living for themselves. Number two, they're going to be pissed as hell because now, they're damn near bald and just made a permanent decision based off of temporary feelings. Hell, I work for you, so I will make it happen!

But I just want people to see the good in themselves and realize that life is what you make it. Lose yourself in goodness, not in bullshit. Women are incredibly strong. As soon as we realize just how strong, women will begin to value themselves more. In this life, if you ever want people to respect your situation, life, or decisions, you have to respect it first. No one will ever care if you don't.

Remember, at some point, right when you have reached that crazy "feel good, this shit is awesome level," someone may come along and do to you, what you have done to others. It's all a standard of wisdom and maturity. Do unto others as you would want them to do unto you. I was recently asked a question by my father-in-law to be, he said;

"If your mother wasn't a wife, and if her mother wasn't a wife... How will you know to be a good wife to my son?" If someone asked me this question 10 years ago, my maturity level would not have allowed me to give an accurate answer, so instead I sat up, and I thought about the truth in his words. I can't speak for men, but as a woman we often mimic the female images placed before us such as mom, aunt or grandma and we began to take on their role as head of household, strong, domineering, loud, boisterous and so on... When in reality, all momma and grandma wanted was a safe, dependable and loyal man to lean on, draw from and rely upon. No one in this life with good sense chooses to be so damn independent that they don't need help. You have to want something different if what you saw wasn't complete. I had an ex tell me "Alesia; you keep this shit up, and you're going to be a sexy-ass lonely woman, a man should never come home and have to wonder who wears the pants" He gathered me together quickly. Again, I was mimicking behaviors that I had seen many times growing up. As women, we always speak about being a wife when an enormous number of us have no idea what it takes. I answered him saying that I knew that there had to be something better than what was seen while younger and that I was willing to create a better image of love.

Chapter 16

I'm Sorry

*I'm not here to judge anyone about the decisions
they make or have made in their life, I happen to be pro-choice
and did what I felt was best for me.*

We arrive. People are outside angrily shouting in loud objection of this very permanent decision. I hold my head up to face what's ahead. The process is long, and the paperwork seems to never end. He holds my hand slightly, in support or guilt. I see the anger in his eyes, but we can't turn back now. We both know that there is no future within us; only a friendship. My name is called. He (the father) looks at me as if to say, "You don't have to do this," but I turn away quickly because, for reasons deeper than him, I did need to do this.

My heart is pounding as if an anxiety attack is about to arise. A still, freezing, room full of tubes, jars, instruments, bed, and a classic gown are all I'm given. "Please remove your clothes," a cold voice said to me. "Place this on, and the doctor will be with you shortly," she continued.

A couple of knocks came to the door, and a tall, white man appeared, fresh-faced and well-groomed. I studied the room carefully, telling myself that I would remember every detail of it because I would never return.

"Lay back and relax," he said. How could I? I was literally having life pulled from me. I recall two tears sliding down my face. One tear was of regret, and the other a small sigh of relief knowing that I would never have to be plagued as a single mother or a baby momma, ever again.

Just like that, it was gone. A piece of my soul that I could never put back was gone.

Just like that, it was gone. A piece of my soul that I could never put back was gone. "I'm sorry," I mouthed to myself as I regained consciousness. I've always been pro-choice, but I realized that had I been a bit more proactive in protecting myself, I wouldn't be here enduring this. We can be careful, or careless, but know that there are consequences to both.

Our lives would go on, he and I, but our life wasn't consistent enough to deal with one another. We parted on a good note. He's a great father to his other children. I went on and continued to do my thing as a mother, however, there are many times that I think about ALL of my actions. All of them. I'm thankful that God still loves me, even through my filth. He finds it possible to love me. My mistakes became fewer after all of this. I started to pay closer attention to whom I shared my time.

Chapter 17

Respecting the Woman I've Become

*Hold your head up high girl. Don't feel sorry for
yourself. Of course, you've made some mistakes. You're
not perfect are you? Once you understand the core issues
of how your own heart works, it will allow you to see
how others feel. Never set your standards so high
that even you can't reach them.*

Here is a simple, little fun fact about Alesia; I have NEVER knowingly been with, dated, or screwed another woman's man. I know some may think it's very hard to believe. You'd be surprised with the amount of crazy rumors I've heard about myself over the years. My life is so clear, that if I had trust me, I would say so! I've been in situations growing up where I could have, but nothing in me would allow it to happen.

This hasn't stopped men from placing me in similar situations growing up. Still, nothing in me would allow me ever to hurt a woman the way I have been hurt. I figured that in due time, they would get what they deserved in life. I've had friends indulge in it, but it just wasn't for me. I haven't had to share anything in my life. My brother and I are nine years apart, so why would I start sharing a man?

Please know, that I don't judge those that have done this. Believe me, when I say I have my shit to answer for. I live my life based on treating people the way I want to be treated. If a person can't give me what I need or deserve, then I move on. Yes, I've been in many relationships; some great, some good, some bad. There were even some that I just shake my head at, but one type of relationship that I haven't encountered is an abusive relationship. Thank God that I haven't met "that guy", the physical or mental abuser.

I'm not a weak woman. I can't be broken down very easily.

I'm not a weak woman. I can't be broken down very easily. It doesn't make me better than anyone; it's the way I was raised. When men say that I "think like a man," I laugh, because, in reality, I feel like any other human being. I don't wear my heart on my sleeve. When animals smell fear, they attack. I'll be damned if I ever become someone's prey. The flip side of that is the fact that my thoughts can also push a man back. He's left feeling as if I don't need him. I can't tell you how many times I've tried to explain how that's simply not true. When a woman says that she doesn't NEED a man, that's a smoke screen. We do, just not always in the manner in which a man may think. We need their love, touch, and time.

I've grown to understand that men also need women to stroke their ego, make him feel like a man, be a freak, be spontaneous, stimulate his mind, and make him feel at ease. I pride myself on being the kind of woman that pays enough attention to her man that I can cater to his desires without him asking. Paying close attention to your mate will reduce a lot of issues. It only becomes a problem when your mate doesn't do the same in return.

Ask any man from my past, and they'll agree that I'm a pretty good woman, but my tolerance level is very short. Why am I single now, you ask? Sometimes I think it's because I just haven't found a man that knows and understands his worth. When an unusual woman is presented to him, he feels as if he doesn't deserve it, or like it's too good to be true. As soon as men start to realize that they are kings, they will become more selective about choosing their queen.

I have to have a man that realizes that I come with a past, a hell of a past at that; a broken, sexual, insecure, and flirtatious past. Fortunately, I am no longer that woman, but it's a part of me. I was convinced not to let a man "get me". I would always "get him" first. It was a mental game that I would play to keep myself from getting hurt. I would hang out with them from time to time, but nothing too much. It was on my watch, that way I could control the situation.

I wouldn't take them to meet friends or family because I needed it to stay fresh with minimal expectations. I didn't allow them to meet my son, and I didn't respond to their kids. There was a guard that I kept up from anyone getting attached. If I laid beside you, I was gone before daylight. There was never a reason to stay and cuddle. If they called, I would appear busy. Should someone happen to come by my job or my crew, I would act as if it was our first time meeting. You know, I work in a salon, and you never know who's screwing who. It was best to keep all contact to a minimum. Just when it looked as if he may have caught a feeling or two, I would disappear.

This went on for years, or at least until I found what would seem to be my match. You know, the guy that doesn't take my shit, pays no attention to my petty games, hardly called, or stopped by. I liked them! That guy would see right through my bullshit ass cry for help and love me unconditionally. We would last awhile; then it would fade to black. I've always been a faithful woman. The games were during my "single" season. One day, I realized that at the end of the day, the only person that was going to bed unhappy was me. Instead of just being a lady, I chose to be and think like a guy. I was under the impression that I was protecting my heart.

Crazy thing, is that none of them were ever even trying to hurt me. I was just afraid of the thought. I've honestly never been through that type of pain. Sure, I've been lied to, cheated on, etc. But shit, after about two days or so, I bounce back.

I've loved, even been in love. I refuse to allow someone to take me to my lowest place. I believe that once a person, male or female, takes you there, it's because you now love them more than yourself. I'm woman enough to say that I was afraid of that. I want and deserve good love; we all do. There are just as many good men as there are real women. You will never hear me bashing men. What good does it do?

People do what's allowed. If you don't like something, leave the situation. No matter what it takes, leave.

People do what's allowed. If you don't like something, leave the situation. No matter what it takes, leave. If your ass doesn't like a pair of shoes, I bet like hell you'll take them back. I'm not saying that relationships are that easy, but God doesn't place us in unhealthy situations and expect us just to stay and deal with it. That's our choice.

Newsflash ladies, men, can be just as unhappy as women. We think that since they're men, they have to be tough all the time. Bullshit. They have feelings too. We tend to label them as weak when they express them. You will soon learn to stop that when another woman starts to appreciate the emotions that he has. You want someone to console your ass when you get down, so does he. I'm not going to tell you anything that I haven't been through myself.

Respect goes both ways. I spent many years not truly appreciating myself, yet I expected others to. Now that I've taken a step back, re-evaluated my life, I'm looked up to by people I've never met. This includes young, old, and especially my son. For those that don't, it's because they are stuck on who I used to be...

Chapter 18

You Can't Please Everybody

Sometimes, just saying the word "no," feels amazing.
Think about how many times you've said "yes", and then to
the first time you said "no" to someone. It's as if you've never said
"yes"! It's impossible to make others happy because it's not your job.
You are only in charge of your happiness. Take politics for example.
I see the world each day ridicule and criticize our presidents and
leaders due to them making decisions that will appeal to our entire
country. I wonder to myself how in the hell can one man please an
entire country? Hell, I know husbands and wives that can't juggle
families, homes, and careers, so please enlighten me on how you
plan to voice an opinion on how you can run the world better. Get
the hell out of here with that. Understand that what may not seem
fair to you, is probably blessing someone else. Sometimes the
word "no" can simply mean not right now. There could
be something much greater in store for you.

People can be so inconsiderate. They expect so much
from you while giving absolutely nothing in return. There are
times when you just don't have it to give. Let's take money for
example. Money has ruined many relationships and friendships.
When a person is asking for the money, they are at your mercy.
They listen to everything you have to say, they explain in details
why they need it. More importantly, they share when and how they
are going to pay it back. Once you give it, in most cases, the tables

immediately turn. They disappear. The calls stop, and they have the nerve to catch an attitude when asked to repay.

Where in the hell was all this "attitude" when you were asking for the money in the first place? How does one find it in their heart to get upset when they know that they owe a person? What I say to people, is don't give what you don't have, and don't loan or give someone anything that will cause financial or emotional strife in your life. It's ok to say no. There is no guarantee that you will receive it back. It's a chance that people take each and every day.

Unfortunately, there are some losses that you just have to take; even friendships.

Unfortunately, there are some losses that you just have to take; even friendships. Real friends understand and communicate with each other. Associates are just that; people who only associate themselves with you when they need something.

The other component is emotions. Believe it or not, some people feel it's totally okay to hurt someone else's feelings. They use the excuse of "just being real", but I call it bullshit! People that live their life like this have no filter or place in my life. Now, there is constructive criticism. It could be misconstrued or received wrong when it isn't coming from a good heart.

Take a look at your close circle of friends. In each group, there should be a leader, lover, giver, and motivator. A taker shouldn't exist in the group. A taker will only bring you down and drain you. For instance, the leader will likely lead you to more positive situations. They'll seek the best and highest for everyone equally.

The lover will find the good in everyone and genuinely want to see you make it in your relationships, family, and goals. The giver is vital because they'll have an incredible mind. Anything they say or does is from the heart. They won't use what they know to throw back in anyone's face. Be careful not to abuse the giver. You never know when you may need a helping hand or even a friend. My personal favorite is the motivator. This individual keeps everyone on their toes, pushes them toward greatness, and believes in you even when you don't believe in yourself. Motivation is needed.

Often, we can become so overwhelmed with our day to day life that we begin to lose sight of what prompted us to move forward in the first place. The motivator keeps the boat afloat at all times. If you're not prepared to have someone give you the ugly truth when it's needed, the motivating friend is not for you. I want someone to challenge me mentally and physically. It helps me realize that failure simply isn't an option in our friendship. Once you've looked around you, identify which friend you are and strive to be better at being that person.

Chapter 19

I Absolutely Did Not:

Ask to be born.

Expect my biological MOTHER to leave.

Ask to be dark.

Expect low self-esteem.

Plan a pregnancy at 15.

Plan to do it alone.

Mean to disappoint my MOMMA.

Want to admit I didn't graduate.

Intentionally seek the wrong men.

Know I'd lose everything.

Know God would give it all back to me!!

Know I'd beat cervical cancer.

Expect to be a top stylist.

Expect to open my salon.

Know I'd be in a position to give jobs to my community.

Realize I'd make people smile the way I do.

Expect my son to graduate.

Know I'd be the dopest mom.

Have any idea I'd write a book.

Take my clientele for granted.

Know I'd meet the best man

Ever feel sorry for me.

Know that life could be this peaceful.

I absolutely did not know that all of those things would shape me into the person whose book you are reading right now...See how my life started off low, and God took me to new heights? Had I not gone through those things, I'd never have a story to tell you all...

Cut and Dry:

I know for a fact that this book will save a life. I'm a living testimony. I want you to know that no one can tell your story like you. Don't allow anyone to take away your voice. It's powerful, especially in the world we live in today. If, at the end of this life, all I've affected is one person, then my job is complete.

I've shared quite a few very intimate details about myself in this book. There are things here that I haven't shared with anyone. Some of you have probably been through or are currently going through similar situations. Below are a few questions for you to ask yourself. I hope that as you answer them, it helps you begin to recognize your greatness and start on a path towards the best YOU.

Have you ever felt abandoned?

If so, how did/do you cope?

Have you ever been abused (mentally, physically, emotionally, etc.)?

If so, have you forgiven your abuser?

If not, why?

Do you hold any grudges?

If no, how's that working out for you?

Do you love your inner self?

If no, why not?

Do you suffer from insecurities?

If yes, name them.

What's your biggest mistake?

Did you learn from it?

Name 3 great things about yourself

Are you ready to live?

It's time to rise above it all, take your life back, and start loving the new you! I use the "concrete rose" analogy because it sums up exactly from where I've come. I started in such a dark place in my life, wandered through grimy filth I put myself in. Left entangled between the weeds (people) in life, it seemed like they were holding me under until I lost my breath. My will to grow was gone; I felt hopeless and empty. But, a force from above broke ground and allowed me to see a beautiful ray of sunlight. It let me know that there was truly a light just ahead of me. As that ray of sun kissed my smooth chocolate roots, I started to feel the strength of a lion. I burst through that hard, cold concrete and blossom into a radiant delicate red rose. The red rose is tied to the goddesses of love Aphrodite and Venus. Its symbolic meaning still reigns as the ultimate symbol of both love and affection.

So yes, I'm very proud to have become the woman you now know, and I will be equally proud to watch you blossom into the same. Your best life is just ahead.

- Alesia Lester

Life behind the Chair

Alesia Lester

50654794R00077

Made in the USA
Lexington, KY
24 March 2016